# THE PATH TO HOME

## The Life of
## Mildred English Folsom

WITHDRAWN

Compiled by her daughter
**Jorette Martin**

∞INFINITY
PUBLISHING

INFINITY PUBLISHING
1094 New DeHaven Street, Suite 100
West Conshohocken, PA 19428-2713
Toll-free (877) BUY BOOK
Local Phone (610) 941-9999
Fax (610) 941-9959
Info@buybooksontheweb.com
www.buybooksontheweb.com

# *Acknowledgments*

Most sincere and grateful thanks go to Margaret Marr, my editor and friend. Her wholehearted enthusiasm for this book encouraged me and her expertise was crucial to the final work. I am forever grateful for the time, energy, and patience Peg invested in developing this book. Without her insightful comments and suggestions, this story might have remained hidden away in diaries and letters or half finished on the computer.

A special recognition and heartfelt thank-you goes to George Marr whose enthusiasm for this project was greatly appreciated. Thank you for being a number one map maker and for help in resolving computer issues.

I am indebted to Peg Ross for tracking down information I was missing and for directing me to the vast collection records compiled by my mother. Peg's wisdom gleaned from being the present town historian proved invaluable. Thank you for your prompt response to my e-mail requests for information.

Many thanks also to Millie Auwarter and Deborah Thomas who provided answers to my questions about the Greene Hospital and to Amy Marsland who clarified issues concerning the revitalization efforts in Greene.

Thanks to Nancy Bromley and the Greene Historical Society for all they are doing to collect and preserve the history of Greene

I am deeply thankful to Randi Walker who helped format the photographs included herein. Without her photo skills, I would have been adrift in a sea of JPEG files.

Thank you, Tom, for your input and your perspective on our childhood. Thank you, Elisabeth, for digging through family photos and sending ones I needed.

And most of all, I owe immeasurable thanks to my beloved husband, Larry, for his patience during my highs and lows that went with writing this book. Larry, you have been supportive in countless ways—you have read and reread these chapters, been my first critic and editor and your grammatical skills indispensable—but what I appreciate the most is that you continued to love me throughout this long ordeal.

Lastly, I am grateful for the love and encouragement of family and friends throughout the process of compiling and writing this memoir. God bless you all.

—*Jorette Martin*

# Contents

# Foreword

This is the story of my mother and the town in upstate New York that she called home. Mildred English's great-great-grandparents had settled in Triangle in 1815 and subsequent generations settled in the Town of Greene and surrounding areas. Mother's ancestors were hard-working farm people who raised their children to respect God and live according to His word. Her life reflected those values instilled by her parents—namely an unwavering faith and a strong sense of responsibility and commitment. Mother's life spanned all but five years of the 1900s. She began compiling this narrative in the hopes that her descendants would learn about their heritage as they glimpse her life.

Most of this biography is taken from letters and diaries my mother kept throughout her lifetime. In a few instances, I have added entries from the diaries of her brother, Paul J. English, to give the reader a more complete picture of growing up in Greene, New York. The first eighty years are mother's own story of growing up before the days of the Internet and cellular phones and include events and experiences she deemed of chief interest or importance. Mother never completed her memoirs, although she continued to be active in the community. I picked up where she left off, filling in the details from 1975 until 1999 when she died at the age of ninety-five.

My task has been to draw together a picture of her nursing career at the Greene Hospital, her activities as town historian, and her parenting skills as a single mom. What I have written here is from personal notes, letters, and newspaper articles that I found among my mother's records. I have included them in her voice. I hope readers will enjoy meeting this remarkable woman whose life is revealed in this narrative.

*—Jorette Martin*

# Preface

Each of us is an original creation of God, put on this earth for a definite purpose, and in some way, we are affected by everything around us and by every person who crosses our path. No doubt we probably also inherit some of the traits of our ancestors, about whom we know so little.

My serious reminiscences of my life began after the Business and Professional Women's Club of Greene selected me Woman of the Year in October 1976 when Millie Pixley asked my daughter, Jorette, to write a brief biography about my life. The surprise of hearing that read at the club's dinner meeting and then seeing it on the front page of the *Chenango American* caused me to look back at the little events that possibly have shaped my life.

I grew up listening to stories about my parent's lives yet never talked much about my own, so how much do my children really know about me or about our family's history? I recall my father and mother telling Paul and me stories about their lives and that of other family members and about places they had visited. I found it fascinating to listen to my elders when we went visiting on Sunday afternoons and I often daydreamed about the places I wanted to see when I grew older.

Reading was my passion as I was growing up. I wanted to know about people and places and history. I read everything I could get my hands on and reread it again if I did not have another book to read. I loved details, so I hope you bear with me as I tell you about the story of my life.

*—Mildred English Folsom*

# Chapter 1

---

# My Ancestors

---

*To me the foundation of American life
rests upon the home and the family.*
—Herbert Hoover

When I first began tracing the origin of my father's family, I enlisted the aid of my father and older relatives to learn as much as I could about our ancestors. I discovered that my first known paternal ancestor, Luke English (1754–1812) and his wife, Mary Prince, settled in Easton, New York, in Washington County before 1790, according to the 1790 census, which listed six boys and three daughters all living at home. In October 1795, Luke bought 170 acres in Easton (a section of the Saratoga Patent, an English land grant) from a Dr. Philip Smith. He is believed to have come from Connecticut and before that from somewhere in the British Isles. Luke died in 1812 at the age of fifty-eight while on a visit to Madison County in New York State. He is buried in the Randallsville Cemetery about forty-five miles north of Greene. Records show that several of his children settled in either Broome or Chenango County.

One of their twelve children, my great-great-grandfather, Nathaniel English Sr. (1787–1836) and his wife Elizabeth Barber (1790–1882) and three children came from Easton to Triangle, (Broome County) New York, in 1815. Ten more children were born to them in the Town of Triangle. Their first deed to 100 acres is dated May 1, 1815. He is buried in the South Street Cemetery in Triangle.

My great-grandfather Frederick (1816–1889) was their fifth child. Frederick was a great horse trader and he knew the law as well as any lawyer. Whenever neighbors had legal questions or troubles, they came to him. Frederick married Maria Eggleston (1814–1891) in 1837. Their six children, four girls and two boys, were all born in Broome County.

My grandfather, Merritt Edwards English, (1844–1911) was Frederick and Maria's fourth child. He was born on what I believe was the homestead in Triangle that was purchased in 1815. He attended the Indian Brook School that his father had attended and where his own children went later. He taught in the same country school earning $4 a week and lived at home. He married Caroline Lowell (1849–1934) on December 20, 1865, when he was twenty-one and she was sixteen. They worked on several farms for two years until he bought the 120-acre Ike Foster farm off the Indian Brook Road, which was partly in Broome County and partly in Chenango County. The farm was in two school districts, so the children had a choice of schools to attend. If they did not like the teacher in one school, they switched to the other.

My father, Maurice Birdsall English, born on April 5, 1877, was the oldest son out of seven children. When he was fifteen years old, his folks moved to Greene. He went to school on Monell Street for one year and then quit school when he turned sixteen. His first job was working in the broom factory for Lester Fairchild. He earned seventy-five cents a day for ten-hour days and worked six days a week. When he turned eighteen, he worked for A. B. Robinson taking care of hogs and calves. Maurice earned $25 a month that year. The year he was nineteen, he owned a meat market in Greene, but due to poor economic conditions in 1896, he ran out of money to pay his bills since one-third of his customers could not pay their meat bills.

For the next three years, Maurice worked on a farm near Whitney Point or stayed at home and worked for his father. He got one-third of all the profits and saved all his money. So in 1899, he bought the Sabin Hayes 127-acre farm on the Triangle Road for $2,500.

These generations of Englishes were farmers who lived a simple life revolving around the land in Triangle, the Indian Brook area, and Greene, New York. My father was also a good carpenter, building a large basement barn when he was twenty-three and numerous other smaller structures on the farms he owned. The wives of these men were daughters of farmers, with the exception of my mother, Anna Marie Justen.

My mother's parents, Peter Francis (Franz) Justen (1829–1913) and Katharina (Catherine) Pauli Justen (1838–1905) were born in western Germany in what is known today as the Rhineland region. They met at a Kermis in Adenau, Germany, in December 1863. Peter Justen (thirty-five) and his brother Michael (thirty) worked at cabinet making in Cologne. While on a visit to their hometown, they chanced to meet the *fine-looking* Pauli sisters Katharina (twenty-four) and Maria Anna (twenty-six) who had come to the church festival from Daun, about twenty miles south. On May 8, 1864, Peter and Katharina were married. Michael married Maria Anna, possibly at the same time. Four years later, in 1868, Peter and Katharina came to the United States on a sailing vessel. With them was their two-year-old daughter, Gertrude. The trip took six weeks and Katharina was sick all the way. Katharina brought with her twelve linen sheets, twelve pillowcases, and twelve linen chemises that she had spun, woven, and made herself, a feather bed, and a spinning wheel. They settled in Albany, New York.

In Albany, my grandfather, Peter Justen, worked for the D&H Railroad Company building the interiors of Pullman cars. In 1872, he was transferred to Oneonta, New York. When my mother was born on November 24, there was an unusually heavy snowstorm. A train had become snowbound, all available volunteer help was sent to dig it out, and Peter was one of the helpers. When he returned home and was told twin daughters had been born, his disappointment turned to anger as he already had four girls. He was sure that "this time" he would have a son. (It was not to be, however, as they still had one more daughter after the twins.) Mama's twin died at birth and she was "buried in a cigar box." Anna Marie was so small that her mother carried her around on a pillow for months. There were no incubators in those days, you know.

From Oneonta the Justens moved back to the outskirts of Albany where they had one cow, a garden, and many flowers. The girls had a long walk each day from their home on the corner of Morton and Delaware Avenues to Our Lady of Angels School well inside the city. Mama minded the cold more than the others did as she was small for her age and her clothing was thin. She suffered chilblains and in later years called her feet her "weather prophets." She had everything from sunstroke to typhoid during her early years. When she began recovering from the latter, she craved a pickle, but of course, no one would give her one. She kept begging until finally a neighbor sneaked a fat dill pickle in to her. Mama said she ate half of it and nothing ever tasted so good. Then she fell asleep with the other half still clutched in her hands. Her mother, finding it, was horrified and expected it to kill her. However, it did not, and she started to improve at once.

Aunt Mary, born in 1870, was the first Justen daughter to marry. She married John Tiernan when she was nineteen. They had six children. Aunt Katie, born in 1868, was left the widow of James Van Deloo when he died in 1893. They had one son, Matthew Justen (who with his wife, Loretta, died in an automobile accident on July 11, 1937). Aunt Gert, who was the eldest, married last, on August 1, 1906 (to Joseph Wolfendale) when nearly middle aged. They had two daughters, Gertrude and Mary. Aunt Carrie, the youngest, married Will Davis but had no children. She died May 17, 1917, at age forty of breast cancer. Anna's three other sisters all died in their late eighties of old age.

My mother, Anna, went to a Catholic school. She had classes in German in the morning and English in the afternoon. Her class was all girls; no boys were allowed. Anna was a very bright scholar. She was the only one of the five who was not a dressmaker. She went to work at age fourteen as soon as she finished school and became a children's governess for a number of wealthy families in Albany, New York City, and Chicago. She taught the children German, English, and good manners. She particularly liked working for Jewish families. One summer in between jobs, she and some girlfriends went to a summer resort hotel at

Maryland, New York, and waited on tables. Another summer, she was persuaded to be the pastry cook at a hotel on Canada Lake in the southern Adirondack Mountains.

Always interested in genealogy, Anna was the only sister to seek out and visit her parents' relatives in Germany, Chicago, Wisconsin, and Greene, New York. In 1893, when she was twenty-one, Anna had saved enough money to travel by train to Chicago to attend the World's Fair and to Wisconsin to look up members of her mother's family. The next year she and two sisters came to Greene, New York, to visit a cousin, Fred Gardner, who lived on the farm that his family had left in 1882 when they moved to Wisconsin. In 1898, Anna went to Germany to look up her father and mother's families in Köln (Cologne), Daun, and Adenau.

In 1900, Anna and her mother traveled to Greene to visit Cousin Fred Gardner and his family for two weeks. Fred's wife, Stella, invited a young neighbor, Maurice English, to supper that first evening. Maurice came and he and Anna were attracted to each other at once. She was twenty-seven, a petite 5 feet 2 inches tall rosy-cheeked brunette, pretty and vivacious, who all her life smelled like violets. Maurice was tall (5 feet 9 inches), dark, and handsome. He had recently bought a 112-acre farm, and was beginning to think he needed a wife. The next day he took her to the Whitney Point Fair—a new experience for Anna— and they laughed and frolicked like teenagers. During the afternoon a sudden, terrific thunderstorm blew down trees, tents, and the grandstand and even killed one woman on the grounds. Papa always knew the right thing to do, so when the sky blackened they fled to their buggy, hitched the horse to it and to the hitching rail, facing into the wind. All her life, Mama was terrified during thunderstorms and this was no exception. When it was over the fairground was a shambles and everyone was bedraggled and soaked to the skin. Only Anna and Maurice emerged from their buggy looking as if nothing had happened. Everyone asked, "Where were you?" "How come you are not wet?"

They saw each other often during the next two weeks and both knew "This is the one for me." When Anna left for Albany, she had promised to marry Maurice.

The next two months were stormy ones for her. No one in her family had ever married a non-Catholic. They did not want her to live so far from the family, nor experience the "drudgery" of farm life! Aunt Gert made the biggest fuss. (Jealous, maybe?) Anna got more upset by the day. She finally wrote to Maurice saying that maybe they had better call off the wedding. No, sir! He wrote that he would be right out there to Albany. She answered by return mail to come for her birthday on November 24 and meet the family. So, out he went and she met him at the train station.

Aunt Gert wasted no time in telling him what she thought and he told her to shut up, that he was going to marry Anna, not any of them, so they might as well become friends and stop making everyone around them miserable. The family was surprised at his determination and they became enchanted with him. All were friends when he left at the end of a most delightful week.

Of course, he had to tell Anna that his neighbors were shaking their heads, too, and saying the marriage would never work, because she, a city girl, would not be able to adjust to the life of a farmer's wife. But Anna just said to herself that she would show them!

The marriage took place on January 23, 1901, (the third time they saw each other!) in Our Lady of Angels German Catholic Church in Albany. Anna and her four sisters had all been baptized, received their First Holy Communion, were confirmed, attended school, and married in that church. Maurice was twenty-three and Anna had turned twenty-eight on her recent birthday. Anna always kept her age a secret, as she did not want anyone in Greene to know that she was older than her husband. Their marriage was a happy one, lasting sixty-four years, and they loved each other to the end of their days.

From the day Anna came as a bride to my father's farm she was a tonic to the whole neighborhood—friendly, always singing (or whistling), and full of new ideas. Her family was determined, however, that she was not to get lonesome "way out there in the country" so no summer ever passed without some of them, their relatives or friends, coming to visit.

Nieces or nephews usually brought a friend, sometimes for the whole summer vacation.

*Maurice and Anna English on their wedding day*

One summer, Anna bought a new hammock with her egg money just before two girls came for a visit. It was completely worn out when they left. Another year, two boys who loved to wrestle spent the summer. One of the boys broke his leg. After the doctor had applied a cast, Maurice made crutches that the boy used all summer. When Grandpa Justen came, he built new cupboards in the kitchen, a bench and a footstool. Grandma Justen was failing in health and Papa would carry her out to a rocking chair on the lawn so she could view the beautiful valley.

It was a busy but happy life and the newlyweds did everything together. Maurice had built a large basement cow barn (36 feet by 66 feet) when he bought the farm in 1899. He had worked all winter cutting down trees for lumber to build a new barn for his sixteen milk cows. Now he tore down all the old buildings on the place and built a henhouse so Anna could have hens and eggs to use for "trading" for groceries. The house sat back from the road and overlooked the barn and the sprawling pastures dotted with my father's dairy herd.

Grandpa and Grandma English and their two youngest children, Vivan (fifteen) and Arthur (fourteen) lived with the newlyweds the first two months in 1901. Then Grandpa and Grandma bought and moved into a small house east of the farm on the west corner of the short connecting road between Route 206 and the Taft Road where Papa's sister Alta and her husband Luther Taft lived. The George Foster family lived on the east corner of this road.

In 1903, Mrs. Foster and Anna became aware that each was expecting a baby in February. I picture them calling on each other frequently. All babies were born at home in those days, and as Mrs. Foster already had two boys, her experience was helpful. Both women were fortunate to have Grandma English living between their houses, as she had not only had seven babies herself but was the neighborhood midwife who assisted at all deliveries.

The night of February 3 came and Anna told Maurice it was time to get his mother and the doctor—in that order. He lost no time in getting his horse and buggy out and racing the three miles to Greene to get Dr. Elliot, who followed Maurice home in his own rig. At 2:30 a.m. on Thursday, February 4, 1904, I was born, weighing seven pounds. Cost of the delivery was $15.00. Gladys Foster was born one week later.

When I was born in 1904 life expectancy in the United States was forty-seven years. Theodore Roosevelt was president and the American flag had forty-five stars. There were 8,000 cars in the country and the price of a new Ford was $850. Only 14 percent of the homes had the luxury of a bathtub and only 8 percent of homes had a telephone. The average wage in the United States was 22 cents an hour, with the average worker earning between $200 and $400 a year. Bread cost 5 cents for a pound loaf, sugar cost 4 cents a pound, and coffee was 15 cents a pound. Eggs cost 14 cents a dozen. Many farmwomen, including my mother, raised chickens in order to sell the extra eggs for a little spending money. Most women only washed their hair once a month, and used borax or egg yolks for shampoo. More than 95 percent of all births took place in the home. Most women did not reveal that they were expecting a child; pregnancy was simply not discussed. The leading causes of death in the United States in 1904 were pneumonia and influenza, tuberculosis, diarrhea, heart attacks, and strokes. Two out of ten adults in the United States could not read or write and only 6 percent of all American adults had graduated from high school.[1]

---

[1] The Year 1904: www.victoriaspast.com/1904/timeofyourlife.html

# Chapter 2

## My Early Life

*A child should always say what's true*
*And speak when he is spoken to,*
*And behave mannerly at table;*
*At least as far as he is able.*
—Robert Louis Stevenson

My mother named me Gertrude Mildred English, after her oldest sister Gertrude, yet I was always called Mildred. Since Mass was seldom celebrated in Greene during the winter months, my mother took me to Albany to be baptized in the family church on Easter Sunday, April 3, 1904. Probably the next time we went to Albany was to attend Grandma Justen's funeral. She died on December 7, 1905.

According to my mother, I never did creep but just hitched myself around the room. Once my mother noticed that I was doing everything with my left hand, yet she knew I was right-handed. She took me to the doctor who found that I had a dislocated shoulder. It may have happened when Mama was dressing me in a long dress that babies wore in those days. Baby clothing was not at all practical, so many children did not begin to walk as early as they do today. I was over a year old before I walked alone.

When I was one and one-half, Charles R. Wheeler, Greene's local photographer, took my picture. My cousin Margaret Tiernan was with us that day and said he had quite a time getting that picture. They stood me in a chair, then beside it, but every time he had the camera focused and the black hood over his head ready to snap the picture, down I would fall, as I was not used to my new slippery-soled shoes.

*My first photograph — Charles R. Wheeler 1905*

The Albany relatives sent a box of Christmas tree ornaments and Papa cut a little pine tree from his woods for my second Christmas. Those ornaments were an artist's dream and lasted through two generations; balls, a star, an angel, tinseled ornaments, and red candles. All of my father's family was there and when the candles were lit, they brought me into the room. They said I just stood there and looked and looked at it in amazement while everyone held their breath. Then I heaved a big sigh, turned around, climbed on Grandma English's lap and fell asleep.

The next major event in my life must surely have been when I fell into a well down near the barn. Papa had it nearly finished and was placing the large flat stones around the top and I was watching him. He turned to pick up another stone, heard a splash, and I was gone. Things happened so fast then that he could hardly remember about it afterward. The well had not yet filled so the water was nowhere near the top. Somehow, he braced his legs and tried to reach for me as I floated to the top of the water. After missing once or twice, he succeeded in grabbing my white dress with his fingers. It was surely only by the grace of God that either of us survived. He carried me, dripping wet, to the house and Mama surmised what had happened. She said he was more shaken and white than I was. And it was a miracle that I had not inhaled a single drop of water! She dried me and put me to bed and I slept the rest of the day. After that, every time I saw the well I would point to it and say "hole."

When my parents did the milking in the early evening I went to the barn with them and soon knew the name of every cow, which Mama had previously named when she first came to the farm. Probably my very first memory is of the big white bull lying down at the far end of the barn, and climbing onto his back. Fearing for my life, Papa pulled me off him in a hurry, as bulls were notoriously ugly and had gored many a farmer to death.

I vividly recall several incidents in 1907. One scene is of Mama setting the dog's dish out on the porch. Fritz was a big red dog and it fascinated me to see him gobble his food. He kept growling as I stood there and Mama told me to come away because Fritz was afraid I would take his food from him. However, I did not move and he snapped at me, biting me through the lower lip. They took me to Greene to Dr. Elliot to have stitches put in, and I never saw that dog afterward.

That spring Papa plowed the big field on the upper side of the road next to the Broome County line. Each time I ride past there today I see little Mildred walking along every furrow with him, back and forth, the entire length of the field. They could not keep me away and I never got tired. When Papa finished he would set me up on the back of one of the horses to ride to the barn.

One day Grandma English took me out to the little A-frame coop behind her house to see the new baby chicks and she let me hold one. But I held it too tight and she had to take it from me. Mama and I must have called on her frequently that spring because Mama expected a new baby in the summer.

Once they missed me and discovered me over at the Fosters among their beehives. I remember peering in one, then in another, people screaming at me from two directions to come away from there. But I paid no attention. Mr. Foster ran to the house and returned wearing a large hat, a bee veil, and long gloves. He led me away from the hives, untouched.

We seldom went shopping in town. Mr. Van Ostram stopped by occasionally with his grocery cart. Mama would let me pick out a piece of penny candy after she finished her shopping. There was a second traveling cart too, which contained notions and housewares. I remember Mama buying a saucepan from a wagon.

Haying time came and Aunt Vivan helped Papa by driving the horses while he pitched the hay onto the wagon. This requires skill as each forkful is placed in the wagon to prevent slipping, first on one side of the wagon, then on the other, from back to front. When the hay is unloaded in the barn each forkful is removed in the same order. One day I was on top of a full load of hay in the meadow below the barn, jumping around to "help" Aunt Vivan "tamp it down." When he was ready to start for the barn Papa sharply told me to sit down or I would fall off. But I did jump once more just as the horses started up and off to the ground I slid. Because that scared him, Papa was angry and told me to "get to the house!" He had never spoken like that to me before. The next scene is a vivid picture: Mama was ironing a pillowcase on a board resting between the backs of two chairs. As I opened the screen door, she asked me, "What's the matter?" I did not answer. She said, "Did your father scold you?" I never said a word.

A neighbor gave me a little black and white kitten with a pink nose, named Topsy, and I wheeled it all around in my doll carriage and it even slept on the couch with me when I took my nap. It came to the door at a certain time each morning and I was there to let it in. I sure loved that kitten, but somehow I was always pretending it was sick and I was taking care of it. So Mama made a little white cap for my head and said I was a nurse.

The day after Mama had picked the cherries from our tree my brother Paul was born—July 19, 1907. I have a vague recollection of someone putting me in bed with Grandpa English and remembering how soft the featherbed was. Probably Papa had taken me there when he went to fetch Grandma. Later I was taken back home to Mama's room to see the new baby "that the doctor had brought." No one needed to tell me that he had brought the baby in the big black bag that was sitting on the chair. News of the new baby spread quickly due to a new telephone line along the Indian Brook Road.

Next day there was a terrific hailstorm, which broke nearly every windowpane in the house. I remember Aunt Vivan holding the window shade down to keep the hail out. I saw my terrified mother lift the baby to the back of the bed next to the wall, and he fell to the floor causing even more excitement. After the storm, our neighbors, the Fosters, picked up buckets full of large hailstones and made ice cream.

I liked to watch Grandma bathe the baby on her lap, the white washbowl on a chair beside her. Once I pointed to the umbilical cord and asked what that raisin was doing on the baby's belly. She could not convince me that it was not a raisin. Then one day it was gone.

Dr. Elliot told Papa that he wanted to retire and was looking for a farm for his son Harry, who wanted to be a farmer. Our farm interested him, so he and Papa made arrangements for the sale of our farm. By September 1, we moved to Albany to try city life. Mama and Papa had lived on this farm for six and one-half years. I was three and one-half years old when we moved. I wanted to take my kitten but

Mama said the kitten would not be happy in a city where there were no fields to roam to hunt for mice.

*The house on Route 206 where Anna came as a bride in 1901 and where Mildred and her brother Paul were born.*

Soon after we moved to Albany, Papa purchased a desirable lot at 352 Orange Street and drew up the plans for a two-flat house. He had already cut logs on our farm in Greene, which he reserved, to build our new house. His father took the logs to a mill in Greene and then sent the lumber by freight train to Albany. When it arrived, Papa sent the lumber to a kiln to be dried. Then Papa started to build the two-story house.

My only memory of our temporary home on Yates Street is of an upstairs kitchen with blue painted walls and a high ceiling, an oil stove with a removable oven, and a table on which set a small can of condensed milk—all different from what I had known. Papa carried a dinner pail to work and I would meet him at the top of the stairs when he came home. His first job was helping Uncle John Tiernan on a painting/paper-hanging job. For a while Papa worked on the construction of the new State Education Building. Aunt

Gert's husband, Uncle Joe, also worked there until a severe injury resulted in the loss of his leg. When he recovered, he was given a newspaper stand on the first floor of the Capitol building, where he worked for the remainder of his life.

During the winter, Papa made a sled with a box on it to pull Paul back and forth between Yates and Orange Streets so we could watch the progress on the house each Sunday. It was finally finished in the spring of 1908. We lived in one apartment and rented the other. I can still see the red roses on the wallpaper in my parent's bedroom, the shiny varnished floors in the new house, and my brother Paul whining as he followed Mama from room to room. Could he ever creep fast!

A retired fire chief and his wife rented the second floor. She liked me and gave me a little blue leather purse with two amethysts in the clasp. It had belonged to her little girl who had died many years before. That first summer a girl from across the street and I watched carpenters build a new house next to ours and we collected pieces of fancy molding discarded by the carpenters to use as blocks.

I remember being very ill with "gastric fever" and for a while, they despaired of my life. The last time the doctor came to see me he stood me up on a chair and put his shaggy gray head against my chest to listen to my heartbeat. Then he set me down in the Morris chair and told Mama that I was well and he would not need to come again. I sighed wearily and thought that I felt no different from before.

Papa carried me a lot those days and I held onto his ear "to warm it." Ears looked like shells to me. Once when we were dining at Aunt Katie's I finished first and left the table to get a better look at twelve-year-old Mattie's ear. I had a toothpick in my hand and stuck it in his ear, he yelled bloody murder and I got a spanking. I guess that ended my interest in ears.

George Kirk, a boy next door had a birthday party to which I was invited. The girls all wore their best and the boys wore their Buster Brown suits. We played pin-the-tail-on-the-donkey and various games until everyone tired of them. Then I said, "Let's play horse." At home I had a long line made of knitted yarn of many colors, perhaps three inches wide, and Paul and I played horse a lot. One would be the horse, the other the driver. With so many children at the party, two could be a team. However, George did not have a rope of yarn. He said, "My mother has some ribbon; let's use that." It was okay with me so we got it from her sewing basket. However, that narrow blue ribbon was very long and got all tangled up, so George cut it. When Mrs. Kirk discovered what we had done, she was angry. She really scolded me and said I should have known better.

At a certain time each day a tinkling bell heralded the approach of the milkman's cart. Every door seemed to open at once as housewives emerged with their containers. Mama had a blue-and-white enameled pail, which the milkman would fill with his long-handled dipper that hung inside the big milk can. Then with a cluck to the horse, the cart would move to the next stop. I also remember the rumble of the ragman's big wagon and his singsong voice: "Any rags, any bones, any bottles today?" And we children would run in and tell our mothers.

I recall watching Mama dust her dresser one day and observing the interesting things on it. Then, tiring, I flopped down on her bed, my head coming to rest upon a sheet of sticky flypaper! Well, did she ever have a time getting me free from that flypaper! As fast as she snipped my hair off in one place more hair would get caught on the flypaper. Shampooing my hair didn't help much either as only more hair would need cutting to get rid of the glue.

The family celebrated Grandpa Justen's ninetieth birthday on November 7, 1909, at Aunt Mary's with all the family present and a group picture was taken. A few days before, Mama mentioned that she must cut Paul's bangs but since she did not get to it right away, I thought I would help her. I got the shears and went to work on him thinking she would be so pleased to see what a great job I had done. Well, when she saw us, she gave a shriek and almost cried. She could not repair the damage because I had cut the bangs up to his hairline!

In December, I saw the most beautiful doll in a store window on the avenue. How I wished she were mine. Each time we passed that store I was afraid she would be gone, and I thought of little else. When Christmas morning came, I was the first one up to see what Santa had brought. Our front room was a fairyland with its decorated tree and presents underneath. There was a little horse on wheels, a teddy bear, and a doll in a little rocker—just like the one I had dreamed about. I picked her up and ran to my parents' room crying, "Look what Santa brought me!" However, a small rug on the waxed floor in the hall slid from underneath my feet and I fell flat on my face and broke that beautiful doll's head. I was heartbroken. Aunt Carrie had made all the clothes including a dress, slip, and panties with tiny tucks, insertion and lace. I had those doll clothes for many years for other dolls but I never forgot my heart breaking when I broke that beautiful doll.

* * *

In February I turned six years old, so Mama enrolled me in Our Lady of Angels Catholic School. I remember watching the children playing in the yard and feeling I was an outsider because I did not know how to play like they did, and was too shy to join in. I have but one memory of the schoolroom. One day a little boy raised his finger and the nun said to wait until recess, but he was very insistent. She grew impatient and made him come up to the front of the room, facing us. He still held that finger up so she shook him hard, which made him cry. At the same time, a big puddle appeared on the floor and then she hustled him out of the room fast. I felt sorry for that boy and thought she should have known what he meant, because even I knew that much.

About this time, in early 1910, Grandpa English wrote that he had bought Arthur Stafford's farm on the East River Road in Greene. Uncle Arthur and Aunt Vivan had married and lived there a year, but he wanted to move to his hometown of Oxford. Grandpa also mentioned a couple of desirable farms for sale in Greene, which at once sparked my parent's urge to return to farm life, where both had been happiest.

*My grandparents, Merritt and Caroline English*

So, Papa took me to Greene for a weekend, and a horse and buggy ride to Aunt Alta's, stopping en route at what later became the Van Slooten farm on Route 206. When we arrived at Aunt Alta's, they were making butter. I remember a cool room off the kitchen with long shelves the length of the room on which set large flat pans of milk waiting for the cream to be skimmed off and churned into butter. Crocks of assorted sizes were stacked underneath the shelves. Later, we always bought our crocks of butter from them.

I remember the delicious breakfast at Grandma English's: sausage, pancakes with sausage grease for them, fried potatoes, and molasses cookies. Grandpa made a big fuss over me, his first grandchild.

Grandpa held me on his lap, tickled my face with his goatee and said, "I hope you'll be a schoolteacher when you grow up, just like your Aunt Vivan." I recall Grandpa's long white nightshirt and the little bottle of wintergreen on his dresser, heavy patchwork quilts on Uncle Arthur's bed, celluloid collars in a translucent box in the top drawer of his highboy, and the bunch of letters there "from his girl-friends."

Aunt Vivan came down from Oxford to see us and told me not to break the colored Easter eggs in the parlor, "which shook" as they would smell terrible. Grandpa's secretary desk and impressive books fascinated me, as did his big swivel chair. His penmanship was the most beautiful I ever saw. Aunt Vivan gave me a shoebox full of ribbons and silk pieces and trinkets such as little girls love. This became my treasure chest but I had to leave it there until we moved to Greene. Then I played with it constantly. She had also cut paper dolls out of Sears Roebuck catalogs including clothes for all seasons for them. How happy I was!

\* \* \*

Papa bought the Van Valkenburgh farm (located on the Coventry Road, one and one-half miles northeast of the village of Greene) as soon as he looked at it, and we went back to Albany to tell Mama.

Papa found a quick buyer for our house and by April 1, 1910, we moved back to Greene. He had to pay the tenants on the Van Valkenburgh farm $500 to vacate it by that date. My only memory of moving was watching Mama carefully pack the dishes in a barrel filled with oats. Papa must have gone to Greene ahead of us because he was not on the train with Mama, Paul, and me. This was the first of several train rides to and from Albany that I remember. Before changing trains in Utica, Paul was sick and vomited all over the floor. Mama paid the conductor to clean up the mess. Papa met us at the depot and took us at once to see our new farm home.

On the way, he told Mama that Grandma English had said we could have her kitchen stove. Mama said, "If it wasn't good enough for her, it wasn't good enough for us," and she wanted a new one, too. And she got it—a shiny new Glenwood Range, about which much of my early life revolved.

# Chapter 3

## Life in the Country

*Isn't it splendid to think of all the things*
*there are to find out about?*
*It just makes me feel glad to be alive*
*—it's such an interesting world.*
—Lucy Maud Montgomery
*Anne of Green Gables*

The new home that I grew to love was in the country, one and one-half miles from the village of Greene, New York. Papa and Mama were excited to return to life on a dairy farm, and this lovely farm was Papa's dream. It was known as the Van Valkenburgh farm and contained about 160 acres when my father bought it. The farm itself dated back to 1832 when Adam Van Valkenburgh bought and cleared the land. The farm became the property of Joseph D. Van Valkenburgh when he returned to Greene after making his fortune in California at the time of the gold rush. He made the farm into a "gentlemen's estate," building a fifteen-room house, in 1871, and using hired men to do all the work. He raised various breeds of cattle including black-and-white Dutch Belted cows, sheep, hogs, and even peacocks and other fancy farm-yard fowls. There were all kinds of outbuildings to explore and beautiful flowers and climbing roses everywhere. Everything on the farm fascinated a six-year-old.

However, once we started living in our new home, it must have looked discouraging to Mama as one day I found her weeping. Every room needed new paint and wallpaper. The dark varnished woodwork had blistered and black creosote had run down the walls from stovepipes in the chimneys. Our furniture, which fit fine in a five-room flat, looked lost in a fifteen-room house with large, high-ceilinged rooms that had no cupboards or clothes closets in them. But worst of all, there was no running water in the house. The well pump was outside as was a small outhouse. The cows drank from a large round tub near the kitchen porch and made a muddy mess between it and the cow barn. And there were no neighbors in sight!

*The Van Valkenburgh farm on the Coventry Road*
*where we lived from 1910 to 1920*

I remember one night that April when Papa came from the barn and called us to come outside the house to see Halley's Comet in the starlit sky. He and Mama and I stood facing north looking at that large star with its long fuzzy tail and he said something about how people feared that if the tail curved downward it would sweep the earth. I wondered how it could do that, but seeing that my parents showed no sign of fear, it didn't bother me either.

For me each day was full of surprises. Imagine taking a bath in a round washtub in front of the kitchen stove with the oven door open. Every day I would catch occasional glimpses of the two beautiful peacocks, pigeons eating with the chickens, and barn swallows up in the peak of the barn. I was fascinated by a litter of little pigs and I loved hearing the sound of peepers in the swamp. I remember a huge turkey gobbler that chased Paul each time he went out into the dooryard. In the spring, the daffodils and narcissus appeared as if by magic along the roadside, and violets and other wildflowers grew everywhere.

Mrs. Hiram Curtis was the first neighbor to call on us. She brought Kent with her, who was my age and had long blond curls. He was as shy as I was and we just stood by our mothers and looked at each other. Mama said Kent was a boy but I did not believe it. Then when we called at their house, his curls were gone. I thought he was a different child, but on the wall hung two oval portraits of her boys, Palmer and Kent, with long curls when each was six years old.

I attended the village school the rest of the term, with Florence Bryant as my teacher. Except for songs we learned, I remember little else other than the two uncontrollable Horton boys and coming down with the three-day measles. While at home, I played with Paul on the back porch. He had a hoop and dropped it in the water tub, and in trying to reach it he fell in. Heavens, how he cried and I yelled for Mama. Soon after that, Papa moved the tub to the back of the barnyard. And before long, we didn't see the turkey gobbler either!

A new sink appeared in the kitchen along with some stationary tubs. Then Papa hired a man to help him dig a three-foot deep ditch 50 rods long, by hand, from the house to a spring far up the hillside and water was piped to the house. The pump and the outhouse vanished after Papa partitioned off the end of the front hall for a bathroom. However, we had a temporary collapsible tub for some time until Mama insisted that Papa install a better bathtub with legs.

There were hooks on a board on the kitchen wall where Papa hung his hat and jacket, and a roller towel on the back of the door. The wood box was behind the stove and there was a swinging door between the kitchen and living room. We did not use the parlor for some time so the dining room became our living room and we always ate in our large country kitchen. Once Papa finished painting and wallpapering the rooms we used and Mama hung the lace curtains, the house became livable. Eventually cupboards were built between the dining room and kitchen.

The round oak stove in the front room was our source of heat until a hot-air furnace was installed in 1913, when Mama received an inheritance from her father's estate. We used kerosene lamps until Papa installed acetylene lights.

Each day that spring, a new variety of flowers appeared on either side of the path leading to an octagon-shaped summer pagoda. A crimson rambler rose bush draped itself around the entrance. There was a bench built around the inside of the pagoda and a round table stood in the center, where I had tea parties with my dolls. I was ecstatic and played there all summer.

A round ceramic umbrella stand was just inside the front hall double doors of the house and outside there were white peonies and a fragrant double white Killarney rose bush. Papa was always bringing us surprises: dandelion greens, horseradish, cowslip greens, and puffball mushrooms. He showed me patches of wintergreen in the "night pasture," and took me fishing in a rowboat on the pond where he would catch a mess of bullheads in no time at all. There were yellow pond lilies there, dragonflies, and an occasional frog on a lily pad. Many kinds of birds flitted from tree to tree around the pond. Papa was really enjoying himself. And, what amazing rainbows and sunsets we saw!

There was a lot to do on that farm. The land was stony and each year after spring plowing and before planting seeds, some 100 loads of stone would be picked off the fields and carted away on a flat "stone boat." Papa was as meticulous about his farm as Mama was in her house. He continuously made changes to the farm such as a new cement floor and stanchions in the cow barn, a new milk house, a henhouse for Mama's hens, and a new silo. One by one, the different breeds of cows were replaced by Holsteins, the hens by white leghorns, and our team of horses was always black. The first winter Papa butchered the hogs and raised no more after that. I do not think he liked pigs.

Paul received a little red wagon for his third birthday in July, so I drew him around in it a lot. One early evening while our parents were milking we played on the steep runway of the horse barn located across the road from the house. In pulling the cart down too fast, I turned too short and Paul pitched forward into the road, cutting his forehead on a stone. Between the dirt, blood, and tears, he was a mess when I got him to Mama. She screamed when she saw him and took him to the house where the injury proved to be smaller than feared.

Papa found that horse barn quite inconvenient so he built an addition on the south side of the cow barn for the horses and used the old building for wagon and machine storage. The woodshed had been the original house on the farm in 1820. The next owner later remodeled it for a garage.

The lane from the barnyard to the foot of the hill, north of the buildings, was a fascination to me, including a little spring where the cows drank. I eagerly learned the name of every growing thing: the black birch tree, the slippery elm, the sassafras tree, chokecherries, as well as names of wildflowers. Along the foot of the hill were two long rows of purple and white grapes. Eventually they died out for lack of care. The Van Valkenburghs had plenty of help for all this diversified farming, whereas my parents did the work themselves, only occasionally hiring a man by the day.

East of the grapes was a wild blackberry patch from which Mama canned about 100 quarts a year besides making dozens of jars of jam. Aunt Katie spent most of her summers with us and was a big help. Grandpa Justen spent his last summers on the farm, too. Mama bought a double-seated gliding wooden swing and I remember them sitting in it shelling peas and snipping beans. Sometimes he would swing Paul and sing German songs. We children pretended the swing was a train and played "choo choo" in it. I guess I was conductor and engineer, and Paul was the passenger.

In the fall, we picked up bushels of hickory nuts from our five trees, and barrels of apples in the orchard, and we always sent one barrel to the relatives in Albany. We had many kinds: McIntosh, Talmon Sweet, Tompkins County King, Northern Spy, Pippin, Strawberry apples, and several other varieties. The huge, oily-skinned, juicy Kings were my favorites and I have never seen any like them since. Papa took the imperfect apples to a cider mill to be made into cider, which we stored in two barrels in the cellar. One barrel was for drinking (while it was sweet), the other for vinegar. They were propped on racks on their sides and each had a spigot in it.

Mama stored hickory nuts in an unused room over the kitchen near the stovepipe. Sometimes, on cold winter nights, we would hear the sound of nuts rolling across the floor because a squirrel had gotten in. The squirrels really had a merry old time with those nuts. Once Mama set some bottles of homemade root beer up there and always at night, the corks took a notion to pop out.

In the late fall there were large chestnuts to be picked from American chestnut trees high up on the hillside. Most had to be knocked off the trees with long poles and the burrs, which still clung to them, had to be hammered off. About 1912, a chestnut blight killed every chestnut tree in the country.

Mama joined a Larkin Club—a neighborhood buying club—that year. I would look at the catalogs, which featured everything from toilet soaps and creams to shoes, wearing apparel, and toys, among other things. I remember the fragrant round cakes of sandalwood and clover guest soaps and the glycerin and rosewater hand lotion that Mama bought. For selling their products, she acquired an oak library desk and a polished oak stand for the living room as premium gifts. That desk held our Bible, maps, catalogs, stereoscope viewer, and pictures and the Volume Library, which I used growing up.

The Watkins man and later the Raleigh man stopped at regular intervals to sell their products to rural housewives. These traveling salesmen sold ointments, salves, liniments, vanilla, buttons, candy, brushes, brooms, and much more.

\* \* \*

In September 1910, I started going to our District No. 15 one-room school, a mile east of our home. This made three different types of school within a few months for me, but it didn't bother me. The teacher, Myrtie Lyman, drove to school and picked me up as she passed our house. She kept her horse at Frank Barton's, the neighbor closest to the school. One afternoon I was waiting for her to hitch up her horse to go home when I noticed barrels of apples (in the barn) that Mr. Barton had just picked. They were shiny red and all the same size. The longer I looked at them, the more I wanted one. Now we had lots of apples in our own orchard, which had not yet been picked, but this was the first time I had ever seen barrels of them. I took one of those apples hoping he would not notice that it was gone. No sooner had I done so than I knew I had done wrong, and because of my guilt, that apple was like ashes in my mouth. It bothered me for years and every time I saw Mr. Barton, I imagined him thinking, "There's the girl who stole one of my apples." That was an experience never to be repeated.

Another incident I remember happened just after Christmas. My parents were doing the evening milking and Paul and I were alone in the house. We played with the ABC blocks and I read my new cloth "Night before Christmas" book to him. I probably couldn't read but I knew what was on each page from hearing it so many times. We were hungry and decided we wanted some raisins, which Mama kept on the top shelf of the pantry cupboard. I could not reach them so I lifted Paul up to get the box, telling him to put his foot on the bottom shelf. He did . . . right into a pumpkin pie! Our hunger vanished at once and we fled to the couch in the front room and pretended to be asleep when Mama came in from the barn. She started getting supper and when I heard her gasp, I knew she had found the pie. She called me, then came and sat down beside me and asked what had happened. I said, "Burglars must have done it. Yes, burglars did it." She said, "Now you tell me the truth. If you do, I'll not punish you, but if you don't, I shall." Somehow Mama always knew what the truth was. I remember her saying that every mother had eyes in the back of her head, put there by God, and I believed her.

Early in February of 1911 and 1912, Watson Watrous, our closest neighbor, tapped our sugar maple trees to the halves[2]. The Van Valkenburgh farm had been famous for its sugar bush but Papa had no time for making maple syrup

---

[2] "To the halves" means to share equally in the product, in this case to share the maple syrup production.

other than gathering the sweet sap from buckets hung on the maple trees and pouring it into tall milk cans. I rode on the big sledge through the snow when he made the rounds of the trees each day. A large metal vat was set up on our property with a fire underneath that burned day and night to boil off the sap. I liked to watch Mr. Watrous stir and skim that boiling sap until it reached the right stage to pour into gallon syrup cans. All the equipment was ours. He did the work. When he moved away that ended syrup making on our farm. Paul and I liked the wonderful syrup on pancakes and on oatmeal or even made into candy and various desserts. Probably few people today know about a neighborhood Sugar Party. The hostess would boil syrup down to the "soft sugar stage" on her stove and serve it with hot baking powder biscuits. Or, if there was fresh snow, we children loved to eat hot syrup drizzled over packed snow. Making pure maple sugar was a lot of work as it takes forty gallons of sap to make one gallon of syrup.

\* \* \*

Grandpa English died in 1911. He and Uncle Arthur were building a silo when the scaffolding gave way, plunging them to the ground. Grandpa suffered a compound leg fracture and internal injuries, resulting in his death a few days later. We rushed over to see him and I was intimidated by the sight of a hospital bed in the living room, the bright red blood on the splint dressings and a nurse in a starched white uniform hovering over him. He wanted me to kiss him but I couldn't. He was white like a ghost and I was afraid.

Later that spring or summer, we went to visit a relative of my father, who lived near Willet. Mrs. Eliza Covey had a granddaughter about my age who lived with her and would soon to leave for California. Before we left, Mrs. Covey brought Gladys' jewel box out to show me all her pretty (perfumed) necklaces and beads. They were beautiful, just like the girl, who had long dark curls, black patent leather slippers, and wore a pinafore over her dress. She was like a picture. Mrs. Covey offered me one of those strings of beads but I said no. She urged me to take it to remember them by but I whispered to my mother that I didn't want it. I could not imagine my grandmother giving away something that was mine, and besides, I was too plain to wear jewelry with my straight hair and calico or serge dresses.

One day when I was about eight, the teacher had a visitor at school so we were all on our best behavior. At recess time I heard her say, "What beautiful eyes she has," and looking around I knew that she meant me. When I got home I looked in the mirror to see my beautiful eyes, but all I saw were two dark brown orbs. All the others in school had blue eyes. So I started praying for blue eyes as I walked the mile home from school each day. I even selected a certain color of blue in the sky and my prayers kept getting stronger. Grandma English was living with us at this time and doing some sewing. She had difficulty threading needles so I did it for her and once she said, "My! You are lucky to have such good eyes. And I thought, "That's it. That's what the lady really meant, good, not beautiful." What a subtle way God has of switching one back on the right track!

I was growing fast and Mama had to buy shoes for me often. Every time she took me to Maloney's Shoe Store, she would tell him what big feet I had for my age. She never knew how much that annoyed me.

Dr. Meacham came regularly to district schools to examine the children. The first time he examined me he told the teacher to write down that I had a goiter (an enlargement of the thyroid gland that often produces a noticeable swelling in the front of the neck). Well, did I ever watch that through the years! Straight hair, big feet, and now I had a goiter. What a mess I was! Even in high school I would never wear a thin crepe de chine blouse like the other girls because I was so self-conscious of my neck. Like many teenage girls, my imagination exaggerated these physical features way out of proportion. I never told anyone how I felt.

Each school day, one of the boys fetched a pail of fresh drinking water from Mr. Barton's well. The pail was kept on the low shelf in the boy's cloakroom on the west side of the school, with a dipper, basin, and towel close by. The girl's cloakroom on the east side was identical: hooks along the wall for coats, and a shelf overhead for hats and dinner pails. We each carried a different-colored small lard pail with our names scratched on the lid. My lunch was always uninteresting: a bread and butter, peanut butter, or lettuce with mustard sandwich, a hard-boiled egg, and raisins or an apple. The four Steins brought a cold boiled potato, a thick slab of homemade bread and a hunk of butter. One little girl, the envy of all, always had a big wedge of pie with her lunch. I remember the time when one of the boys returned from "going after water" during school hours. He was so hungry that he sneaked into the girls' cloakroom and took that little girl's pie. What a howl she made at noon. As all evidence pointed to him, he finally admitted taking it.

Once the Ladies Aid Society had an all-day meeting at Mrs. Packard's to sew for some fire victims, and the schoolchildren were told they could buy their lunch there for 15 cents. Well, those kind souls hovered over us and stuffed us so full of goodies that we were not good for much the rest of the afternoon.

Another time our neighbor, Mrs. Pratt, was to be alone for the night so she asked Mama if I could stay with her. The next morning she put up my school lunch and it was enough for a working man. She included fried chicken, pickled beets, a real sandwich, cheese, and pie. The kids all hovered around me at noon, drooling, so I shared it with them. As time went on, hot lunches came into vogue and our new young teacher heated cans of soup on the little round stove during winter and doled it out to us.

I have a snapshot of us taken in the schoolyard with Miss Lyman the first fall. She told us to "look pretty." I looked around at the other children who (I thought) were all thinner than I was so I sucked in my cheeks for the picture. In June, before leaving the district, a second picture was taken. My hair was long by then and in two braids. I still did not look like the others, but I did have a beautiful lace-edged handkerchief in my pocket. I gathered the four corners up so all the lace would show and held it up in front of me like a nosegay so people would look at the pretty lace instead of me. However, my hand moved a bit resulting in a white blur in the photo.

*District School No. 15 - Miss Myrtie Lyman and her students*

By 1912, I was in the fourth grade and liked everything but arithmetic. I was constantly looking up words in the big Webster's Dictionary and stood up longest whenever we had a spelldown. Countries of the world on the large globe intrigued me also.

Outdoor games played were softball, tree tag, and "stealing sticks."[3] In winter, we brought our sleds and rode down the long, steep hill south of the schoolhouse during the noon hour. On warm days, we waded in Wheeler Brook north of the grounds and watched minnows and crayfish. The teacher took us on nature hikes and we planted trees on Arbor Day. One year, we gathered thousands of tent caterpillar egg masses from around twigs and in the crotch

---

[3] Stealing sticks was played as follows:
The field is divided into two parts by a well-defined line. At the center end of each side, five or more sticks are placed in a pile. The players are divided into two teams and are scattered over their own side of the field. The object of the game is to steal the opponent's sticks without being caught. As soon as the player crosses the center line, he may be caught and put in prison. A player can be released from prison if one of his teammates can touch his hand. He can then come back to his side without being tagged. The team who gets all the opponent's sticks and has all its members safely out of prison wins the game.

of branches to destroy the egg masses before the caterpillars hatched. Then we burned the eggs and the person who collected the most received a prize.

For a number of years I was the only girl to walk to school from my direction so I got a lot of snowballing from the boys. Then when Kent Curtis drew me to school on his sled one day the others teased me unmercifully. Somehow, instead of hating them, it made me hate Kent and when the teacher told me to sit with him one day to use the same subject from which to draw a picture, I refused. Another time she told him to sit with me but I jumped up and stood in the aisle beside my desk. She didn't know how miserable my life would be if I had sat with Kent. Those big boys would have rolled in the aisles with glee.

One day the teacher received a supply of Colgate toothpaste samples that she doled to us with a pledge card to sign that we would brush our teeth daily. A pledge was a sacred vow to me and I would not skip brushing my teeth for anything. About the same time, sticks of penny candy were being sold with a free ring on each one. How exciting! We girls traded constantly, a ruby for an emerald, an opal for a turquoise, etc. The rings did not last long as they bent easily and the stones came out.

My father was elected Trustee or Collector, 1911–1918, and once I attended a School Meeting with him in my schoolhouse for I wanted him to see my neat desk and the clean blackboards. From 1913 to 1915, he hired Mabel McGowan to teach. She boarded at our house part of that time, paying Papa $3 a week for room and board. Miss McGowan was a good teacher, teaching us manners and correcting our speech constantly. One spring morning as I walked to school with her I took a deep breath and said, "My, doesn't that smell pretty." I was probably referring to the locust trees. Her answer was, "Things look pretty but smell good." The way she answered me made a lasting impression.

She told my father that the school needed library books and gave him a list of books to order. No one was more excited than I when the box of books arrived: *The Little Lame Prince, Pinocchio, Hans Christian Andersen's Fairy*

*Tales, Wilderness Ways, Little Brother to the Bear, Star Land, Greek Heroes, Man without a Country,* etc. The books covered subjects of interest for all eight grades. Paul was not yet in school, so as soon as I had read a book, I took it home and read it to him as he played on the floor with his toy soldiers. One day I took Paul to school with me. I watched over him like a mother hen, but in spite of that, he got hit in the forehead with a ball bat during the noon recess. He started school in 1915 when he turned eight years old.

I remember those school days in 1914 and the neighbor children in School District No. 15. My schoolmates were Eorie, Mary, and Frances Murtaugh; Mary White; Gertrude Badger; Echelene Knickerbocker; Arthur, Anna, Agda, Astrid, and Lilly Stein; and Palmer and Kent Curtis. The school officers were C. R. Pratt, trustee, Hiram Curtis, clerk, and my father, Maurice English, collector.

We made calendars and bookmarks for our mothers for Christmas, Valentine cards, and pictures, learned many poems and skits for a party, and had a picnic on the last day of school to which parents were invited. One year, we invited the pupils from an adjoining school district to be our guests and it was a big event for us. My parents made a five-gallon freezer full of ice cream for the occasion. I had to read "Curfew Shall Not Ring Tonight." At the saddest part, my voice suddenly broke with emotion and I paused to gain my composure. I could sense that the parents all felt for me and at the end, they gave me a long ovation.

I remember winters on the farm, undressing at night by a register in the front hall, leaving my clothes on a nearby chair, then in my long flannel nightgown running up the stairs in my bare feet and down the hall to my room. Mama would already have placed heated soapstone wrapped in a towel in my bed so it would not be icy cold. In the morning, I would run downstairs and get dressed over the register. Paul always slid down the banister.

People burned wood in those days. During the winter, trees were cut down in the woods and drawn to the dooryard where Papa, Rollin Pratt, and Hiram Curtis would buzz the logs into stove-length chunks to be split into stove wood at his leisure. Then they piled the firewood in cords and left it to season until spring when Papa would stack it neatly in the woodshed. Papa furnished the district school with wood and Paul and I helped pile it.

Will Drachler worked in the woods for Papa in 1914 and one day he cut his foot with the axe, right through his heavy boot. He drove the team up to the house where I watched Mama apply first aid. We had no telephone then so Papa had to drive to the Curtis farm to phone for Dr. Chapin who came at once and sewed up the wound.

Another winter job was cutting ice on the Van Valken-burgh pond and filling the icehouse. The "Drachler boys" (Charles and Will) had the ice-cutting equipment and all the neighbors got their ice there. It was a busy scene with teams of horses hitched to big bobsleds coming and going. (I seemed to be the only child to watch everything.) The men placed a layer of sawdust between each layer of ice until the icehouse was filled. That ice would last us a year: for daily use in the milk house vats where the filled milk cans were kept between milking time and transportation to the milk station, for the wooden "ice box" in the kitchen and for ice cream freezers all summer. One thing we always had to remember was to empty the water pan underneath that icebox.

It must have been during the winter of 1916–1917, when Mama and I went to Albany to see Aunt Carrie in the hospital following breast cancer surgery, that Charlie Drachler fell into the pond while icing. Papa and Will Winchell pulled him out as he clung to a large piece of ice and sent him up to our house at once. Agnes Winchell was taking care of Paul while we were away so her husband was helping Papa. She found dry clothes and got him thawed out, and he suffered no ill effects.

We always had a dairy of twenty cows that Papa milked before breakfast and again at 5 p.m. before supper. A lane north of the barn led to the night pasture but the day pasture was a short way up the highway to which one of us would go to let down the bars so the cows could come down the road to the barn. The cows would always be waiting at the gate because Papa did the milking at exactly the same time every day. When we moved to the Juliand farm in 1920, the cows had a wooded hillside to wander through so Papa trained a dog to go after them. He would put two fingers in his mouth and give a tremendous whistle and call "Cum boss, Cum boss" (at least it sounded like this) and say to Buster or Rover who would be jumping excitedly around, "Go get the cows, fella," and away the dog would race up the hill and round up every last one of the slowpokes.

Immediately after breakfast Papa would shave. Sunday mornings after the chores were done, he would put on a white shirt and tie, and no unnecessary work was ever done. That was the Lord's Day—a day of rest, to have company, to go for a ride, or visit friends or relatives. He was not a churchgoer but Mama always took Paul and me to Mass once a mission church was started in Greene. Papa only went to weddings and funerals, and to Christmas and Easter services, but he always said grace at the table. Papa's family attended the Baptist Church when he was young but since Mama was a Catholic, he chose to read his Bible at home.

Hiram Curtis was the first one on our road to have a car—an EMF touring car—probably in 1912. That summer Aunt Gert and Aunt Katie came to visit us and as Papa was unable to meet them at the depot, Mr. Curtis offered to go for them. Aunt Katie had been train sick and could not get to our place fast enough and Aunt Gert was frightened each time he speeded up the car. Between one telling him to hurry and the other telling him to go slow the entire one and one-half miles, neither enjoyed her first automobile ride.

That winter Papa decided he would like a car, too. He said he had never smoked so actually owed himself enough money to buy one. So, in May 1913, he bought a Model T Ford in Norwich and Mr. Curtis went with him to drive it home. When Paul first saw it in the unused horse barn, the car was covered with mud, as there were no paved roads, but he said, "Gee, but that's a beauty!"

Our first ride was to the cemetery on Decoration Day. I sat in the backseat with Mama and it felt as if we were just flying along at 10 or 15 miles per hour. As we neared the cemetery, a lumber wagon was rumbling along in the middle of the road ahead of us and the man standing in it driving the horses did not hear the car. When we were almost upon him, Papa yelled loudly, "Hey! Get out of the road." I said, "Blow the horn, Papa. Blow the horn!" He had forgotten that he had a horn. The man jumped and quickly turned the horses to the side of the road. I remember wearing a pretty blue-plaid dress that day, which Mama had made for me for Easter, and a new straw hat with a bunch of lilies of the valley sewn to the ribbon hat band. Owning a car was a special event in our lives and we dressed up for the occasion.

*Out for a ride in Papa's new Overland Car*
*1914*

The Fourth of July was celebrated with homemade ice cream, of course, and a variety of fireworks: sparklers with punk to light them, Roman candles, skyrockets, and firecrackers of different sizes. I was eight years old when Mama allowed me to shop alone for the first time. I rode to town on the milk wagon and went to Potter's Fair Store where Mr. Potter helped me select the variety of firecrackers that I wanted.

The first summer we had the car in 1913 we drove to Albany and returned via the Helderberg Mountains, going four miles up and five miles down. The radiator boiled over going up and we all got out of the car several times to wait for it to cool down. I don't know how many times Papa had to crank that car to get it started. Finally, we reached the top of the hill with only him at the wheel, the rest of us walking. The radiator was empty so we stopped at a farmhouse where they told us that their well was nearly dry and they couldn't spare any water. It was easier going down the mountain but as it was nearly dark we stayed overnight at a small village inn.

Paul and I had to sleep together at the inn and not long afterward, we developed an itch, which we thought must have come from the bedding. Paul only had that itch one summer but I had it for seven years. I remember Aunt Katie washing us with baking soda water, buttermilk, and finally a salve prescribed by Dr. Chapin. Nothing helped me and I was in utter misery. My winter serge dress fairly drove me crazy and when it was outgrown, I never had another wool dress. Grandma English mixed up sulphur and lard, which was the only thing that ever helped. I carried a little jar to school and used it on my elbows and knuckles when necessary. It started improving during high school but when I entered nurses' training in 1921, I still took a jar with me just in case. But I never needed it. The seven-year itch was gone!

My cousin, Justen Tiernan, from Albany, spent every summer vacation with us until he married, and he helped Papa with the haying, mowing, raking, cocking the hay, loading the hay wagon and driving to the hay barn where the hay was unloaded into the haymow. Mama drove the horses on the hayfork and I kept the men supplied with lemonade. When haying time was over, we took many rides over the country roads to Cortland, Ross Park, Ideal Park, Watkins Glen, Niagara Falls, the Adirondack Mountains, and longer trips to New York City and Washington, DC. Usually Aunt Katie was with us, sometimes the Pratts or Curtises. Whenever we planned an overnight trip, Justen stayed home and did the chores—living in the country was more than enough vacation for him. We always took along food to eat and seldom ate at a restaurant. Rest rooms were unknown so we would watch for country schoolhouses with their outhouses. We enjoyed many a picnic at nearby lakes: Lily Lake (now Chenango Valley State Park), Petonia Lake, Echo

Lake, and Lake View. Occasionally we'd have a tire puncture or blowout and would have to change tires, and someone always came along and offered help. Those were great days— the best of times. Everyone was friendly, helpful, and trustworthy.

The Drachler boys (Charlie and Will) had a threshing machine that they took to every farm in the area when the time came to thresh oats. Neighbors exchanged works. Mrs. Curtis helped Mama cook for the hungry crew on the day they were at our farm and again for two days in the fall when it was silo filling time. My job was to wait on table. Then Mama would help her when the gang was at the Curtis farm.

Astrid Stein was my best friend and lived some two miles up the Coventry Road. One day during Easter vacation, I asked Papa if I could ride one of our horses up to see her. Lacking a saddle I had to ride bareback and the horse walked every step of the way. It was not very exciting! Coming home was different! The horse pricked up his ears and took off on a run. After bouncing up and down a few times, I bounced off onto the ground, right in a muddy rut. I ran after that horse as fast as I could run yelling "Whoa" at the top of my lungs. I thought he was running away, not heading for home, and I was sure Papa would be angry. Lynn Chalker happened to be near the road and knew at a glance what had happened. He caught the horse and held him until I got there, and offered to help me back on, but I said, "No, I'll lead him home." I never rode one of our horses again.

Christmas was always exciting, with Papa's relatives present. The house had to be spic and span, same as for Easter. I'd wash and iron all my doll's clothes and set the dolls under the tree so Santa could see how well I took care of them. I would leave him a note and a cookie and he answered with a note. The last time the handwriting was my mother's. I just couldn't believe it—I guess I matured slowly. For years, I had wanted a doll carriage. Then one day in Potter's Store, I saw just the one I had dreamed of, so I bought it for a dollar. However, when I put my doll in it, I realized that I was too old to play with dolls. After that, I only looked at them. One day Kent came over to play with

Paul when I wasn't around. Later, when I walked into my room, I saw that things were not as I had left them. The boys had played doctor and operated on my favorite doll, which happened to have a cloth body. They had sewed her up with black thread. I was furious as my room was my Inner Sanctum and was off limits to everyone but me.

Probably in 1913, Papa's cousin, Charlie Lowell, from Cortland visited us and invited us to a Methodist Camp Meeting at Lily Lake. He had an active part at the camp. Before leaving, he knelt beside his chair and prayed for us all. Other members of the Cortland clan came with him and brought me a bunch of their Sunday school papers, and I read every one. Their religion was different from mine. I knew many Bible stories, but my catechism lessons were nothing like their interesting classes.

Lois Smith, who was about my age, slept with me that weekend and it did annoy me that she insisted on a completely dark room with all four window shades down, whereas I loved to see the stars and moon shine in. But I did like her prayers. One was *"There are four corners on my bed, there are four angels overhead: Matthew, Mark, Luke, and John. God bless me and the bed I lie on."* Her favorite Bible verse was from the Book of Ruth: *"Entreat me not to leave thee, nor to return from following after thee. Your home is my home and your God my God."*

Then we attended the Camp Meeting. Justen was with us and we and the Cortland cousins sat in the middle of the large tent. Well! That certainly was a new experience: people giving testimonies, crying, wailing—and all those Amens! It was positively scary and I thought they were demented. Suddenly Justen burst out laughing and that started the rest of us kids. We tried to stop and then he would laugh again, and none of us could stop. Ushers told us to quiet down, and finally had to put us out. The next day they kept us out. However, Justen, who was a few years older than I, always remembered two songs that we heard that day. Every summer after that, he would sing them while working in the hayfield or getting the cows. One was *"The Stream of Salvation Never Runs Dry"* and the other *"Give Me That Old Time Religion."*

Reading was my passion. Our newspaper ran continuing detective stories and I read every one: Sherlock Holmes, Charlie Chan, and other stories. We took the *American Agriculturist, Women's Home Companion* and *McCall's Magazine.* I could hardly wait for each month's issue with its serialized story. In the summertime, I'd go to the roadside mailbox to pick up the mail. If a new magazine arrived, I would sit right down on the stone steps by the front door and read it.

When I was eleven, I subscribed to *Moving Picture Magazine* and went all out writing to actresses I had seen in the movies, and some I had not seen, asking for their pictures. And all sent one to me. I brought brown art paper and mounted each picture carefully, all the same size, and hung them on the walls in my room. The room looked like a picture gallery and I was very proud of it and kept it like that until we moved away in 1920. I wrote to Elsie Janis who lived in a restored mansion on the Hudson and she sent me several personal snapshots of herself in her home, in her boudoir, fishing on the Thames, etc. Elsie acted in a handful of silent era films and wrote for motion pictures into the earliest days of sound films. I had some Mavis Talcum Powder, which I would shake into envelopes and shake out again, hoping that would make my letters smell nice.

Silent movies in Greene were first shown at the Old Opera House and the balcony was our favorite place to sit. We kids thought it fun to sit in the first row and drop peanut shucks on the people below. Papa drove the fringe-top surrey the one and one-half miles to town for the 7–9 p.m. show until we got the car. In 1915, the Milfred Theatre was built and a weekly serial was shown which was so intriguing that we simply couldn't miss it, regardless of weather or road conditions. There was the *Perils of Pauline,* the *Exploits of Elaine, The Million Dollar Mystery,* etc. At this theatre people munched on popcorn. Occasionally, after the show Papa would treat us to a soda at Rebecca Elliot's Ice Cream Parlor next door. It was a great day when silent pictures turned to talkies, but for a time we did miss the piano playing that always accompanied the silent films.

Between 1910 and 1920, there were many tramps throughout the country and many stopped at our house for a drink of water, a meal, or asked to chop wood to get a little money. My mother never turned one away. She let them sit on the back porch and rest while she quickly prepared a tray of food for them.

Jack Green, an Albany acquaintance, drove up from Florida once with a load of bananas and spent a few days with us. He made willow whistles for Paul and me. Papa bought a string of his green bananas and hung it in the cellar. Paul and I kept watch of them and ate them as fast as they ripened, until Mama discovered it.

The Greene Fair was the event of the year and rural pupils always had exhibits there. Once I got a silver thimble for my darned socks and a prize for my homemade bread. My pride and joy was a layer cake with maple icing and hickory nuts on top. I was heartbroken when I went to the Floral Hall and saw it looking as if it had measles, as every nut had disappeared. Oh, how upset I was with the people who had eaten those nuts!

An event that everyone talked about occurred when the telephone line was put up on our road. Our phone hung on the kitchen wall and a "short and two longs" was our ring. Everyone on our road was on the same party line. Some neighbors loved to listen in on other people's conversations but Mama told us that was impolite. She firmly said, "What others say on the telephone is not our business."

Box socials, shadow socials, and pie socials were frequent in our neighborhood and there was a lot of good camaraderie. There would be music, singing, dancing occasionally, games and refreshments, and children as well as adults all had a good time.

Washing the dishes and dusting were my regular jobs. Up at 8 a.m. on Saturday, my first task was to clean my room. That was no effort because I never let it get messed up. My clothes were in neat piles in the dresser and everything just so on top of the dresser. If anything was moved one inch from the way I had it, I'd know it. When I finished, I would read a book until Mama was ready for me to dust the downstairs rooms. Then I'd read some more until it was too dark to see. We never lit the kerosene lamps until dark.

When I was old enough I had to get supper every night while my parents did the milking. Supper consisted of warmed up leftovers: fried or creamed potatoes, cold meat or scrambled eggs, homemade bread, pickles, applesauce, cookies or doughnuts, and tea. One evening as I sat before the kitchen range with my feet in the oven, I got so absorbed in the book I was reading, that I lost track of time. I read many biographies at this time and became lost in stories such as E. T. Cook's *The Life of Florence Nightingale*. When Mama came in, tired and weary, and found no supper started she lost her temper. "Put that book away," she said sternly. I knew meals had to be exactly on time but I had neglected my responsibility.

After years of saving her egg money, Mama bought an upright piano and arranged for Mrs. Charles R. Wheeler to give me lessons. I remember the day I was to take my first lesson. Dinner was on the table and I was upstairs getting dressed. Mama called and I said, "In a minute." She called again and I said, "I'll be right down." Then Papa called and I knew he meant it. I said, "I'm coming," but Papa did not wait. Up the stairs he came, razor strap in hand, gave me three belts across my bare shoulders, and said, "When you are told to come, you come." I got my dress on in a hurry but cried all through dinner, hardly eating a thing. I wonder if he was annoyed because he had to drive me to Greene for something he had no more interest in than I. Mama was the one who should have taken lessons, as she was the musical one and I was not. After a year of weekly lessons, she knew it was a waste of her money and our time and so I stopped taking piano lessons.

One day, our neighbor Rollin Pratt had an emergency appendectomy. The doctor performed the operation on their kitchen table and Mrs. Pratt hired a special nurse to care for Mr. Pratt. When Sunday came she wanted to go to church, but it was winter and Greene's mission church only had Mass once a month, so she asked me to go with her by train to attend Mass in Oxford. On the way, she told me about her best friend who was getting married and how badly she felt that she could not attend. She said it was because the wedding would take place in a Protestant church. I asked, "What difference does that make?" She informed me that Catholics are not permitted to attend Protestant church services. I could not believe it! Was that being Christian? Most of our friends were Protestants and my mother had been a sponsor at six or eight baptisms, not all of our faith. Although a devout Catholic, Mama was also liberal minded and I determined to be just like her.

One Saturday Paul and I went over to play with the Curtis boys. We raced around outside and in and out of the barns and I thought, "How silly this is; it's not a bit like playing games at school." Then Mrs. Curtis seemed to sense the situation and asked me if I would like to help her pick up apples. After finishing that, I started back to the boys but she had other things in mind to show me, until it was time to go home. The thought came to me that I was now too old to play with boys yet too young to go out with them. It was an in-between age so I withdrew into a little fantasy world of my own. I became the heroine in all the stories I read and I changed the plot, the conversations, and even the endings to suit myself.

At the beginning of the fall term in 1915, Miss McGowan told us to write about what we had done during the summer. A week later, she had us write about our summer vacation. Since I had already written it in detail the first week I did not do the second paper. In class, she asked me to read mine aloud and was angry when I said I had nothing to read because there was nothing to write about. She made me stand in a corner the entire afternoon to think of something. I cried the whole time with my right arm up over my face. When school was out my eyelids were puffed and I could hardly take my right arm down. That shoulder pained me for months, but I never told my parents. (Moreover, I did not write the paper!)

Another day, before our country entered World War I, she told the boys to pretend they were American soldiers in France writing a letter home, and the girls to be nurses. Therefore, I became Bertha White and wrote gory details about riding out to the battlefields to help ambulance drivers find and pick up the dead and wounded. I concluded by saying, "I just love it." Miss McGowan shuddered when I read my letter and said, "Oh, you wouldn't love it; you couldn't stand it." I meant I liked being helpful. So I said again, "Oh yes, I would." When she repeated her former words, I thought to myself, "I'll show her someday that I can stand it. I will be a nurse." So perhaps she influenced my life more than I knew.

In the spring of 1916, Aunt Carrie invited me to spend a month or so with her in Albany when I went there for my First Communion at the family church. Uncle Will had an antique shop on the first floor of their Washington Avenue house and the living quarters were on the two upper floors. This was a new way of life for me and I loved helping him dust the interesting things in the shop. Then, while attending the Convent School, I came down with measles and was confined to bed to a darkened room because light might damage my eyes. I was sorry that I never had another opportunity to visit Aunt Carrie again because she died in May of 1917.

While I was in Albany, Papa and Ed Sanford, Greene's oldest Civil War veteran, built a veranda around two sides of our house. In the summer, it was a lovely place to sit and read. Of course, when they put the railing on two years later, it added character to the house as well.

When I was in eighth grade, our teacher took me to the village library where I was enchanted by all the books and thought I would read every one. Mrs. Summers, the librarian, showed me the children's section where I started reading the fairy tales from other countries. About the third time I checked out some of those she said, "My! You must like fairy tales." Well, I never took out another one of those. I switched to boy's books such as Horatio Alger and Boy Scout books that were even more interesting, and I read them aloud to Paul. Later on, some of my favorite books were *Anne of Green Gables, Anne of Avonlea,* and *Rebecca of Sunnybrook Farm.*

Uncle Arthur belonged to the Red Men's Lodge and when they had a dance up in their hall, he would invite my parents. People took their children with them, as babysitters were unknown then. It was there that I learned to dance the two-step, the waltz, and square dance—with Uncle Arthur. He was such fun and so very graceful.

# Chapter 4

## My High School Years

*Life is sweet because of the friends we have made,
and the things which in common we share.*
—Edgar A. Guest

Finally the time came for me to leave the district school and attend Greene High School. I loved every day and wanted to learn everything. I walked one and one-half miles to town every day alone with an armload of books and spent the evenings doing homework.

Greene High School

Except for special events like a dance or the School Fair, there was no time for Campfire Girls, Girl Scouts, basketball, or boyfriends because I lived out of town. Oh, I did have a crush on a red-haired boy for a couple of years. He wrote me notes in German, which I kept in a little covered basket on my dresser. During final exam week in 1918, he even gave me a box of chocolates.

I remember the day when it was my turn to speak in Morning Assembly. We could select a poem or whatever but we could not read it, which I preferred doing. I chose a poem by Henry Wadsworth Longfellow titled "The Psalm of Life"

Tell me not in mournful numbers,
Life is but an empty dream.
For the soul is dead that slumbers,
And things are not what they seem.
Life is real, life is earnest,
And the grave is not its goal,
Ashes to ashes and dust to dust
Was not spoken of the soul.

Imagine selecting that at age thirteen! Is this what the real me was like? The poem spoke to me that the soul is eternal and what I do in life will affect the condition of my soul.

In high school, I remember we girls began to wear camisoles as we started to mature. We wore the tightest kind of camisoles to hide our busts. Corselets preceded corsets, which had garters attached to hold up our stockings. I used to wear long underwear in the winter. Mama never knew that I would roll up the legs before I reached school, so they would not be seen through my black stockings.

During winter months, I wore high arctic boots, in milder weather, rubbers and gaiters. Ladies fur hand muffs were in style in those days. Mine was a beautiful black caracal muff made from the fur of a small lynx from India. It kept my hands warm, so I never minded the cold or damp snow. Often schoolchildren were the first to break knee-high snow on the road. Unless I got a ride on a milk wagon (or sleigh), I never accepted a ride with anyone. Years later Ralph Watrous told me how sorry he was for me trudging along to or from town, but not once did I ever ride with that dear man. My mother made a big thing about "riding with strangers." I knew all the resident's names on the Coventry Road and Page Brook Road but to me they were strangers if they did not happen to be in our own circle, which included a neighbor or relative.

In 1916, there was a polio epidemic and the schools and other public places were closed. Only a few people in Greene got polio but one classmate died. When the Spanish influenza epidemic came in 1918 all my family were sick at the same time. Dr. Chapin showed me how to take temperatures and I had to report to him by phone every day. I did everything he told me to do and did not get the flu myself. There was no help to be found to help me, as everyone was too busy caring for his or her own families. Thank God, Mr. Curtis did the milking for us twice a day. I was heartbroken when Uncle Arthur English died in October, leaving three small daughters. He was only twenty-nine years old. Some of my classmates also died at this time as did all of Greene's nurses. By the time the epidemic had run its course, more than 90,000 New York residents were eventually afflicted and more than 12,000 people perished.

On a happier note, at the end of June in 1918, I was invited to the fourth annual Greene High School honor student's banquet at the Sherwood Hotel. It was given by the businessmen of Greene and was a most happy occasion. To be eligible a student had to have an average of 85% or better for the entire school year. I had an 88% average. Of the sixty-six eligible students, sixty-one attended. I was so happy to be one of the twenty-two junior high school students to be recognized for our achievements.

* * *

My brother Paul was frequently sick or hurting himself. When he was about one and one-half years old, he had the whooping cough. He fell into a water trough when he was two and one-half years old and was nearly scared to death. When he was almost nine years old, he fell nine or ten feet through a hole in the barn floor and was nearly killed. Then when Paul was nearly ten years old, he fell thirty feet down a hay chute in the Hibbard's barn (a neighbor) and was knocked unconscious for several days. He landed on his head, nearly breaking his neck, and was confined to bed for two or three weeks. Following that incident, he developed a nervous twitch, which he never outgrew. When he was eleven, he had his adenoids and tonsils taken out. Mama was always worrying about him because he was small for his age and had one cold or childhood disease after another.

During World War I, students had Victory Gardens at home. After school, we high school girls would gather at the parish house to roll bandages and make pads and layettes. During the summer, we enrolled in home nursing classes and completed various 4-H projects. People did without many things such as sugar and flour, and learned to live with hard homemade rice or rye bread. How happy everyone was when the war ended on November 11, 1918! It was a day to remember. On the eleventh hour of the eleventh day of the eleventh month, an armistice with Germany was signed and the cease-fire came into effect. From then on, that day became known as Armistice Day.

On April 23, 1919, Greene had a tremendous Welcome Home Celebration for our local servicemen. Eighty-six men went to war and eighty returned. It was a perfect day; the village was decorated with flags and banners. There was a crowd of more than 3,000 people in town who witnessed the parade, attended church services in the morning and dances in the Opera House and Red Men's Hall in the evening. It was the greatest celebration ever seen in Greene.

I was part of the red stripe in the *service flag* for the six men who had lost their lives overseas. I made my own gauze costume. As we marched up South Chenango Street, my petticoat came unbuttoned and fell to my feet. I simply reached down, yanked it off, rolled it up, hid it under my arm and kept on marching as if it were an everyday occurrence. Probably only the girls on three sides knew it. Later, I was in a British dance and did the Irish jig and wore cut-down green sateen pants and top that I had also made and a big high-crowned hat.

A couple of weeks later, we went to Albany. On May 4th, Paul received his First Communion and both of us were confirmed at Our Lady of Lourdes Church. I was selected to read the prayers.

On June 24, 1919, I graduated from junior high school. My average was 90%. There were twenty-two students in my ninth grade graduation class. I wrote the class history. The Honor Students' Banquet was held the night before at the Sherwood Hotel. I wore my new white georgette dress, the first store-bought dress I had ever owned, and black patent leather high-heel slippers. My long hair was up in a bun for the first time. The boys had also changed overnight—from knickers to long trousers, and somehow everything was different after that night. Our class motto was "The elevator to success is not running. Take the stairs." Looking down through the years, I see this fifteen-year-old girl standing in front of her class on the Opera House Stage reading the history of her class and am amazed at her calmness. What happened to her shyness and the inferiority complex I thought she had? Is that really the same Mildred I know?

\* \* \*

Now that I was fifteen, I assumed more responsibilities at home when school was not in session. Occasionally I helped Mama with the laundry. Washing clothes was hard work because everything was done by hand. First, I sorted the clothes. Then we boiled the white clothes in a copper boiler on the stove and added bluing to the second rinse water. The colored clothes came next and finally the dirtiest ones using the same wash water. I had to scrub the clothes on a washboard with strong yellow soap to remove the dirt. Then I rinsed the clothes in cold water. After wringing them out, I hung the clothes on lines outdoors to dry. This was very hard on the arms and fingers and my back would get sore from bending over. One day I got such a big blister on the knuckle of my left thumb that Mama had to finish. I don't know how she did it all those years—she frequently had split fingertips from all her labors.

I remember two parties at our farm to which more than thirty high school friends came. My mother bought a Sonora, which is like a Victrola, in Binghamton. She paid $75 for it and she bought eight records as well, so we kids could dance to music. Some of the girls played the piano and we all sang.

One of the parties we had at our house was a mock wedding, which was hilarious. There were all girls except for Paul, who was the ring bearer. Papa was the minister and I was the best man. I dressed in boy's clothes as did a few other girls who came dressed as a fellow to fill out the wedding party. The "bride" wore a lace curtain for a veil. Charlotte Macomber, an eleven-year-old girl in Paul's grade was flower girl. Paul had a crush on her and he and Charlotte danced twice. One of the games we played was Winkum. First, you have to wink at a girl and then when she jumps up out of the chair she is sitting in and sits down in the chair ahead of you, you have to kiss her. Once the boys sat down, the girls were to wink at the boys. Charlotte winked at Paul but much to his disappointment, she did not kiss him. You can imagine all the laughter resulting from our pretend guys and gals. We didn't get to bed until half past twelve. I remember Paul saying, "Gee, but I had a nice time!"

The kids all liked my parents because they joined right in with the fun. Mama was a great singer and Papa could recite dozens of long poems he had learned in his school days. So there never was a dull moment. Papa was always the parent to drive a bunch of us to another girl's home. Once we went on a hayride to Smithville Flats. It was a cold night but we had plenty of blankets in that lumber wagon, and sang all the way. There we had hot chocolate at a restaurant before coming home.

At the beginning of the second semester of my junior year in high school, I was called to the office. The principal told me, "Mildred, if you take one more half-year subject (civics), you can graduate in June." Rather than thinking this was good news, I was depressed. Leave all my class-mates whom I loved to graduate with a bunch of older seniors I scarcely knew? But of course, I always did what I was told.

\* \* \*

In December of 1919, Papa sold our 160-acre farm where we lived for nearly ten years. The former J. B. Juliand farm at the east end of the village was for sale and at the same time Mr. and Mrs. H. B. Faroat from Smithville offered to buy our farm for $10,000. Our new farm at the head of Washington Street overlooked the village of Greene. Walter Winston owned it (although people referred to it as the Juliand farm) and Papa bought the 154-acre farm for $12,500. Once the sales were finalized, we got ready to move away from the place where we had lived so happily for ten years (from April 1, 1910 to March 1, 1920). Paul hated to move as his best friend, Kent Curtis, lived just down the road and he did not remember living at any other place.

*Our new home on Washington Street in the village of Greene that Papa and Mama owned from 1920 to 1943.*

In February, Papa started moving a load of furniture and other things in his lumber wagon to our new home. The Faroats also brought wagonloads of their belongings and stored them in rooms that we were emptying until moving day arrived. I remember my parents wallpapering the first floor rooms before we moved to the new farm. J. B. Juliand had the house built in 1875 on a portion of the Lewis Juliand farm. Imagine how I felt about living in an upstairs bedroom that had a bullet hole in the floor where J. B. J. had shot a dog!

Our house was only a half mile from school, so I was able to walk home at noon for lunch. That first noon hour went so fast that I barely made it back to school on time. One Friday noon as I was hurrying home I slipped on a patch of ice on Washington Street that was covered by a thin coating of snow and fell flat on my face. My eye turned so black that when I finished eating, I could not go back to school.

Subjects I remember taking in high school were: 4 years English, 2 years German, 3 years French, 2 years homemaking (cooking and sewing), ancient and American history, algebra, geometry, biology, civics, advanced botany and elocution. My schedule was always full and I often worked on homework until late in the evening. My grades were often the highest in the class, but that was due to a lot of effort on my part.

Now that I lived in the village, there was a flurry of invitations from boys for dates. But it was Lent, the six-week period when I had pledged to give up things I liked best such as candy, gum, ice cream, dessert, movies, and dances. One night a boy asked me to go to the basketball game and dance that followed. I had not "given up" games but I told him the dance was out for me until after Easter. He did not understand that but he took me anyway and brought me home as soon as the game was over. Then he went back to the dance. After Easter, I seldom missed a game or a dance. Mothers chaperoned their daughters back then and they all sat together in the front row of the Opera House balcony. Another advantage of living in town was being able to go to the movies twice a week. Papa and Mama liked the movies as much as Paul and I did and we could walk from our house to see the movies in less than ten minutes.

There were twenty-three in my graduation class in June 1920. We did not have a class picture, nor go on a class trip, but I did have a class pin. I do not remember one thing about the ceremony. I wonder why I completely blocked that class out of my mind. I guess it was because I had no memories of being a part of the group.

Within a week Mildred Corke, Aileen Hurlburt, and I decided that since we were sixteen we must go to work, so my parents took us to an employment agency in Binghamton to see what work was available. We were given jobs at once, they as ward maids in Binghamton City Hospital and I as cleaning girl in the Graduate Nurses Home next to it. I saw them only at mealtime and on our day off when we went home. I roomed in a barracks-like building adjoining the Laundry where my new roommate worked. Most of the women rooming there were patients from the State Hospital who worked in the laundry.

I enjoyed my work and the nurses liked me but I was a fast worker and would be finished by 2 p.m., then did not know what to do. Therefore, one day I went to the superintendent of nurses and asked if she had anything else I could do. I will never forget how surprised she was! We visited and she learned that I wanted to be a nurse as soon as I was old enough and she wanted me to consider Binghamton City Hospital.

For a few days, she had me houseclean the second floor corner private rooms in the hospital. These beautiful suites were saved for celebrities who were able to pay $7.00 per day. They had more windows, drapes, and even a chaise lounge in them.

Each day as I worked a man outside one of the windows on a ladder kept watching me no matter which room I was in and it made me a bit nervous. He was either washing windows or fussing with the flower boxes, and he tried to be friendly. I could not ignore him and he probably learned more about me than I realized, especially my love for flowers. He told me he would bring me a bouquet for my room, but he didn't. The day I finished those rooms he said he was finished also, and he would give me the flowers he had promised if I would meet him that evening over near the ambulance station. I said okay and went over. It was near dusk and he was sitting on a chair. Well! He tried to get me to sit on his lap! I was thunderstruck, pulled away from him and got away from there in a hurry—without the flowers. I had obviously forgotten Mama's advice about not to trust strangers. This experience proved that the Lord is certainly ever with me.

On the very heels of this, the superintendent asked me if I would like to make dressings in the maternity pavilion. I said, "Yes!" That is where I spent my afternoons for the remainder of my two months. Sometimes she asked me to run a dust mop over the floors and proud young mothers would let me look at their brand new babies. I knew this was the life for me. With the $30 I earned those two months, I bought a new Jantzen bathing suit, an umbrella, and a camera.

While I was away, Papa bought a new six-cylinder Nash car and traded in the Overland. The Nash was a dark blue, five-passenger touring car. One weekend, the family drove us three girls back to the hospital and three other people went with us as well, so we found out we could squeeze nine people in the car. Oh, was that fun!

Back home again in September, I learned that my geometry and American history Regents papers had been marked down and I would have to repeat those two subjects for a term, so to prolong the school day I added French III and was I glad to be back in school. This was the second time my geometry paper had come back, which did not surprise me, as I had always hated math, but history? That was a favorite subject and I just could not believe it.

In January 1921, twelve of us girls formed a *Five Hundred* card club to meet twice a month at each other's homes. This was fun and the parties varied: for St. Patrick's Day, Valentine's Day, April Shower or May Day, Halloween, a pajama party, and a progressive dinner with favors, decorations, and refreshments after the card game. Occasionally we would invite boys. I remember a hayride to the Cohoon farm near Coventry, a dinner dance at the Red Men's Hall with a local three-piece orchestra, and a box social at my home. Frequently an out-of-town girl would stay all night with me but I remember only twice staying at any other girl's home.

By the end of January, I had taken my final exams and passed American history, French III, and geometry with a score of 80. So school was finished. I occupied my days with sewing two chemises with crocheted yokes and crocheted edging around the bottom. One of the teachers tried to persuade me to enter Teachers Training Class during the second term, but I was not interested in teaching. However, after thinking about it for a few days, I applied for admission and decided to continue to take French and read books in French. I went to all the basketball games where the Teachers Training Class sold peanuts to get money for a camping trip in the summer. My social life was filled with dances, movies, many dates, club meetings, and I enjoyed life.

In February, I received a letter from the Albany Hospital saying I could enter in September even though I would not be eighteen until the following year. Uncle Joe had met Dr. George Beilby (a thyroid specialist) at the State Capitol and had told him about me. Dr. Beilby sent me a most encouraging letter about the Albany Hospital, its advantages, etc. I answered him at once and said my one drawback was being underage. He gave my letter to the hospital superintendent. That pleased my parents very much. Within a week, I mailed in my application. How plainly God's guidance could be seen in all this!

Teachers Training Class held little interest for me. Perhaps I was the only one of the fifteen young women who had no interest in becoming a teacher. After just two teaching assignments, I knew that teaching was not my forte. However, I enjoyed the friendship of the girls and we made plans for a summer outing. One of my classmates was Genevieve McCombs from Smithville, who sixteen years later married my brother Paul.

In early June, I received an official letter of acceptance from the Albany City Hospital Training School for Nurses. I was so excited. Right away, I set to work making my uniforms. I bought nine yards of double-width sheeting for eight aprons ($4.95) and nine and one-half yards of pink chambray for uniforms ($4.75). I shrunk the material for the aprons and began to sew. I had them all done in two weeks. The collars, cuffs, and bibs were to be furnished by the hospital.

The long-anticipated Teachers Training Class camping outing was at the end of June. We stayed at a camp at Echo Lake for a week. I took the finished aprons along to make the buttonholes and sew on the buttons. We wore our middies and bloomers all the while we were there and rolled our stockings below the knees. We loved the "Trails End" cottage and had a great time swimming, rowing, and hiking. A team of two did the cooking each day; another team did the cleaning. Mrs. Anna Noone was our chaperone. One night we had a party and invited the neighboring young people. Some were real clowns and we had a hilarious time. The following week our W.O.S. Social Club camped at the Gray's Cottage at Lake View. Aunt Emma Gross was our chaperone. We called her "Aunt Em."

The summer went by quickly. I ordered a trunk and carefully picked out what to take with me to Albany. Papa bought me a wristwatch. On August 31, Mama, Paul, and I took the train from Bainbridge to Albany. The next day, Mama, Aunt Katie, Anna Strube and I went to New York City on the Hudson River Boat Line. We did a lot of sightseeing and returned on September 4. It was a wonderful trip. Three days later, after visiting relatives, Mama took me to the Albany City Hospital where my nurses' training began. Little did I dream that this day began forty-six years of nursing for me!

# Chapter 5

---

# Nurses' Training

---

*Sow a thought and you reap an action;*
*sow an act and you reap a habit;*
*sow a habit and you reap a character;*
*sow a character and you reap a destiny.*
—Ralph Waldo Emerson

On September 8, 1921, my new life began. There were seventeen of us "Probs." Some of the girls were several years older than I. My room was 536 on the fifth floor of the Nurses' Home. We had to be up at 6 a.m. Breakfast was at 6:30, followed by prayers at 7:00. Our first class was from 8:30 to 9:30. Lunch was at 12:30 and dinner at 5:30. The first day was spent in orientation to our new surroundings and getting settled. The next day, we learned to make a bed. My first duty consisted of being sent to Pavilion F to take care of the mental patients.

Three days later, three other Probs (probationer) and I were put on the female ward. We had to make beds, fold linen, set up and carry trays, clean the utility room, etc. One day I had to put new labels on the chart rack in the Duty Room. I sat at the desk intent on my work and hardly noticed the retinue of doctors who breezed through the room to wash their hands. Well! What a furor that caused! The superintendent of nurses called the supervisor to her office to find out *who* the probationer was who did not stand up for Dr. Bedell. What kind of an instructress did I have who did not make it clear to her students that we had to stand for doctors? When I was questioned about my rudeness, I said I didn't know he was a doctor and he didn't even look at me. After that, I stood for every V.I.P.

My next assignment was to make an open bed instead of a closed one. I had the bottom and draw sheets on, and then paused to remember how much of the top sheet should be folded over the blanket. An old colored lady in the next bed was watching me and told me exactly how to do it and how far to fan the bedding toward the foot. I thanked her and was her special pet from then on. The supervisor hated blacks and resented her being on the ward. She ignored her shamefully, which made me more attentive to the poor soul and I learned a great deal from her. She taught me to be observing in many ways. "Pillowcases must always open in the same direction, honey, and every stand and bed in the ward must be in exact line, and every window shade the same height." Every day she insisted that I take one of her peaches, pears, apples, or whatever, which her visitors had brought her. "I know how hungry girls can get in the evening," she would say. Perhaps it was she who made me a perfectionist from the start, which I am sure, made an influence on my life.

On September 20, I had my first half-day off. I cleaned my room and sewed. My pretty slips with the crocheted yokes did not come back from the laundry although everything had name labels attached. (I had not considered doing my personal laundry so I learned the hard way.) Lil Betters had not shrunk her uniforms at home, so after they were washed she could hardly get into them. Doreen and I went to a movie show in the evening but had to leave before it ended in order to get back by 10 p.m. when the doors closed. We had to run to make it.

On Sundays, I went to 5 a.m. Mass at Our Lady of Angels Church. I would take turns visiting Aunt Gert, Aunt Katie, and Aunt Mary's family on my half-day off.

One afternoon two of us went shopping over on Central Avenue and I bought an alarm clock. The clerk wound it to show that it worked. A local theatre was showing a movie we wanted to see so in we went, with that clock ticking away in its box. Then in the middle of the show, the alarm went off. By the time I got the string untied and the box unwrapped, the alarm had stopped. Oh, was I embarrassed! Nevertheless, we laughed all the way back to the residence.

One day there was a tonsil clinic and I was sent to the Detention Room to watch the children come out of ether. That was one busy day! A few days later, some of us girls went to the movies. Suddenly my head began to itch like fury under my hat. As soon as we got back to our quarters, one of the girls got a fine-tooth comb and found six lice in my hair. A furious shampooing cleared that up.

My first three month assignment was on Pavilion G, (communicable diseases) and I was quarantined there for Christmas. I remember receiving an electric iron from my cousin, Margaret Gabriel, and was I delighted. At home, we had to heat our flatirons on the kitchen stove. I enjoyed the delicious stuffed baked potatoes and all the ice cream we could eat so much, and as a result, I weighed 138 pounds at the end of my assignment.

In February, I had my first month of twelve-hour night duty on the male ward—a forty-bed unit with two recovery rooms. (Three years later, I would be in charge of that ward.) I was so unsure of my capabilities that I prayed my rosary every night, during free moments, for Divine Guidance. After lights were out, I was constantly making rounds of the ward and once found a patient deceased! I had given him his bedtime medication and he appeared all right but on this particular check, I noted that he had not changed position so I checked his pulse and found him cold. This was my first experience with death and I was shocked. I phoned the intern at once. As we stood beside the bed a fifteen-year-old boy in the next bed who was taking this all in reached out his hand and held mine tightly—without saying a single word. That gave me just the strength I needed—as if God had actually touched me.

I remember a pneumonia patient in the Recovery Room who was very ill and I was told to force fluids down him. This was before penicillin days when most pneumonia cases were fatal. The window was kept wide open (no matter how cold it was) and a draft sheet on his bed kept the wind off him. His temperature was high so we kept an ice cap on his head. I spent every free moment sitting beside him keeping him covered, forcing fluids like no one could later believe, and emptying his urinal. His recovery was a real miracle.

Once I had a young fellow from the penitentiary who was dying. He begged for water incessantly, which came up as fast as it went down, and I practically specialed him. His guard sat outside in the hall and slept whereas he could have helped me. My heart really felt for the boy. He died after I went off duty.

One patient always addressed me as Sister, so I asked why. He said, "There are two kinds of girls, one you call Sister, the other you call Kid—and you are the sister kind." Looking back over the years, I see that most of my patients have been males. Perhaps I've been led in that direction. Once a supervisor said I could be trusted, that she did not have to worry about me, and I took that as a compliment. My mother's advice to me when I left home was to obey the Ten Commandments and the Golden Rule, and never do anything away from home that I would not do at home to cause them any heartache. And Papa added, "Keep boys at arm's length from you. Trust all men a little but none too much." Grandpa English had told his children to learn to say NO—which is sometimes hard to do. I thank the Lord for all this advice.

Pavilion F was an interesting experience: all neuropsychiatric patients, drug addicts, and alcoholics. I remember one woman who was found in her slum room downtown half-starved and literally alive with body lice. Three of us nurses, dressed in O.R. gowns and gloves, stripped her and put her in a tub of warm water to soak the first layer off. The water was black and left a six-inch ring of lice around the tub. This was followed by a second and a third tub bath before we even dared touch her to wash her and cut her hair short. When we finished she looked human and slept like a baby.

One young drug addict was a hero of World War I and had a Croix de Guerre medal. Another once-brilliant lawyer had deteriorated into a mindless, gluttonous animal that no female nurse could handle.

One Sunday morning, I was on duty on the women's floor with a probationer named Trudy Truax. She was hard of hearing so was serving the trays and I was carrying them to the patients. I looked through the small window in the door of one of the locked rooms and the patient in there, who usually talked incessantly, was quiet so I unlocked the door to set her tray inside when like a tiger she sprang at me. I yelled for Truax, who did not hear me. The Lord gave me superhuman strength at that moment as I pulled away from her clutches, thrust her from me, and locked the door in a hurry. Truax stared at me when I got to the kitchen and said, "What happened to you?" My cap was off, my long hair hanging loose, bib and collar ripped half off, but I was only scratched. After that, I worked down in the men's section and Truax was let go.

From May until my vacation in September (1922), I was stationed at the TB Camp at the west end of the city. The ambulance took me back to classes at the hospital and I became errand girl for the patients. In one of the men's bungalows, I had my first experience with bedbugs! We got rid of those bugs in a hurry. I liked caring for the seventeen children best. I played with them, told them stories, took them for walks, heard their prayers when I tucked them in bed at night, and even made them lemonade and sandwiches for bedtime snacks. They sure liked me! However, I soon had to stop the liquids at night because of bed-wetting that resulted. Once I took the children across the lovely nearby golf course. I heard "Fore" yelled occasionally but thought nothing of it until finally a man yelled to "get those kids off the green." So we headed for the clubhouse where I was told the danger we had been in and that the links were off limits to TB patients. It seemed that I learned everything the hard way.

My parents took me to Niagara Falls on my first vacation, to Watkins Glen on the second, and to the Thousand Islands on my third. Those vacations were such a contrast to the long twelve-hour shifts at the hospital, and it was so good to have time with Mama and Papa.

\* \* \*

My second year consisted of floor duty in semi-private wards and children's wards, and in the laboratory. In the spring of 1923, I was the first in my class to be assigned to the Operating Room. The other O.R. nurses were all seniors and one in particular made my life miserable. Maybe it was harder for me because none of my training so far had prepared me for surgery and for the idiosyncrasies of surgeons. However, I did make it. Moreover, when I was at the Brady Maternity Hospital in October, Dr. Donhauser was called in to perform a Caesarian section and he asked me to assist *him*.

I was the last student from the Albany Hospital to have maternity training at the Brady Maternity Hospital and Infant Home of Albany. This was because the Albany Hospital's O.B. load had increased so much that it was no longer necessary to matriculate with other hospitals. Students came to the Brady from Boston, Plattsburgh, Troy, and Rutland, Vermont. My first day on duty at the Brady was in the nursery. We had a demonstration on how to bathe a baby with special attention given to eyes, ears, and nose. I had never handled a newborn baby and I was expected to have fifteen babies bathed, dressed, and out to their mothers by 9 a.m. When 10 o'clock came they were not ready, although I was hurrying as fast as I could, not skipping one of their ears and eyes. I never even thought of bypassing those details. The babies were all hungry and crying and I was crying as hard as they were. The supervisor came to see what the matter was and helped me finish. She did not sponge them. She just held the baby under the warm water spray, dried and oiled him, and said to skip details unless they were needed. So each day got easier. The obstetrician who gave us our lectures said I was the first of his students to get 100 on the final exam.

One summer evening in 1923, another student nurse and I took a walk through Central Park to see the flowers. At home, we would take rides over the country roads before dark and for a moment, I felt a bit homesick. Then toward us came a big shiny black car with two young fellows in it. They looked at us, passed by, and then backed up. "Hi, girls," the driver said, "Would you like to go for a ride?" We looked at each other, then told them that it was nearly dark, that we were student nurses and had to be in before 10 p.m. They promised to get us back. Well, it was a nice car, the fellows looked okay, so we got in with them, she with the blond in the backseat, I with the dark-haired driver, and away we went down the New York highways. This was great, I thought. Suddenly the driver turned down a dark lane and stopped. This I had not expected and told him so, but he had other ideas. After a bit of struggling I grew panicky, then suddenly heard my voice crying aloud, "Father in Heaven, help me!" Now I had always talked to God and Jesus but never as Father, except in the Lord's Prayer. To this day, I believe that the Holy Spirit spoke through me—as my mind had not had time to think those words. Nevertheless, they were magic words. The driver just looked at me amazed, then turned and started the motor and four young people rode back to the Nurses Home in utter silence, each with his own thoughts. My thoughts were that "fine feathers don't necessarily make fine birds." But who knows? I hope that this incident may have affected the life of that young man.

We had lots of fun all through training, with monthly dances, all chaperoned. Each class took turns decorating the hall and making the refreshments. We invited our own escorts, usually medical students. There were long walks, city sightseeing, a corn roast, swimming at the YWCA, roller skating at a city rink, theater, and shopping on our free half days. In winter, we went ice skating in Central Park and tobogganing on a steep slope near the penitentiary. Prisoners inside the barred windows watched us and looked forward to our coming, and would keep us informed of the time so we would not be late in getting back to our home. They would urge us to come again and probably envied our freedom.

Evenings we would gather up in Mabel McCreary's room to relate the events of the day, read, write letters, and curl each other's hair. We would share boxes of goodies from home or make egg sandwiches and orangeade with eggs and oranges each one of us had smuggled off the wards. Mabel was from Canada and had taught school prior to nursing. Since she was the eldest, we always went to her for advice.

She, Nora Shea (who had been to business school), Lillian Betters, and Tyl Bollman were my closest friends from the beginning.

One night Marian Ault took me to her mother's home in the city. After an enjoyable evening playing cards, we retired—but not to sleep! Mosquitoes had got in while the lights were on and nearly drove us crazy. We spent the entire night battling them with swatters. Swarms buzzed around us and while she chased them around the walls, I stood on the bed and swatted those on the ceiling. I pictured how this would look in a movie and began to laugh and soon we were both doubled over with laughter.

Janet Meehan also lived in the city and would occasionally take me home with her for dinner. She spent part of her vacation at my home and went to Watkins Glen with us. She wanted to eat all the time we were traveling. (My family never ate between meals and when out riding there was so much to see and talk about that we seldom thought of our stomachs.)

At a dance early in our senior year, Janet invited Gene Galvin, a medical student, to be her escort. We always had dance programs and filled them with the young men's names. In that way we got to dance with each girl's escort, and he likewise got to dance with every one of us. There never were wallflowers and we all had a good time. This is how I met "Gal," as we called Janet's friend. And he fell for me! We went together for the next two years and he invited me to his Nu Sigma Nu and Phi Sigma Kappa fraternity dances. We double-dated with another couple, went to Mt. Marcy TB Sanitarium where one of his buddies was stationed, and drove to see Indian Rock Art in the vicinity of Syracuse together. Once after going for a ride, we stopped at a restaurant to eat, and when we started to leave found that someone had stolen the starter coil out of our car!

Another time we went to a dinner dance at the Hampton Hotel with two other couples. One fellow had brought a flask of liquor with him. I was strictly against drinking so this was a new experience. I simply said, "No, thank you" and that was it. He finally passed out and we had to take him home. That was an embarrassing situation for all of us.

* * *

My last year of training began in January 1924 with public health work. I was assigned to the South End Dispensary where I would be given a list of places to visit in the morning with directions how to get there and what I was to do. I had to phone headquarters from a store in between each case so they would know where I was at all times. At noon, we would try to get back to the dispensary for lunch, and then start out on the afternoon visits. This was a real education as I had a great variety of cases and everyone was so appreciative. I taught young family members how to bathe a new baby and infirm elderly persons, how to irrigate ears. My enthusiasm really inspired teenage girls. I remember getting into some strange places in the slums, including a house of ill repute, another where whites and blacks were co-habiting (this was not done in those days). But I was never afraid—my uniform was my protection. Moreover, the policeman on that beat patrolled back and forth, past whatever house I was in, for added safety.

This is how I described my second week of Visiting Nursing in a letter I wrote home. "I've traveled from one end of the city to another and back again, and all over in between, so am very tired when 5 o'clock comes. We have to be down at the Guild at 8:30 a.m. where each of us is given her patient list. We go into all kinds of homes and I am learning how to take care of people who do not have anything. We learn how to improvise and each day we have more confidence in ourselves. One day it rained and I got soaked to the skin. My umbrella did no good as the wind turned it inside out. I meet people of all nationalities and am beginning to know the city pretty well, and which streetcars to take. I have even been to Rensselaer and Castleton. I think I'll be a tour guide!"

I enjoyed my two months in public health work so much that I wished I could do it all the time. We visited various clinics, an open-air school on top of a building, and a home for incurables near Kenwood. That was pathetic! Just a few words spoken to the patients made them so happy, as they have few visitors. When we left there, we were all glad that we had two legs and two arms. Our supervisor at the

Guild said she was sorry to see our group go, that we were the best bunch of girls she'd had during her six years there. I got 100 on my exam.

By mid-February, Miss Donald, the supervisor of nurses, began to impose stricter rules. The staff began by getting stricter about lights out at 10:30. A few of the girls lost their late leaves for two months. One night Helen and Katie went to the office to ask for extended late leaves. Miss Donald asked where, when, and how they were going and with whom they were going and then said that 10 p.m. was late enough for any girl to be out—and they could not go. The girls were furious! They had their dresses all ready and their dates were coming for them, and it was the first formal dance to which they had ever been invited.

At the end of February, I went down to the office to ask for Monday off to go home for a long weekend. Miss Donald said "No!" because she was putting me in the diet kitchen. When she saw my bags, she ranted and raved for fully five minutes. Oh, was she mad! And I was so angry that I just cried. Ever since I entered training, I would get weak all over just seeing her coming toward me and whenever I talked to her, the words just choked me.

My work in the diet kitchen consisted of making gelatin, custards, white sauce, and putting up diabetic diets three times a day. Our six-hour shifts were all morning and from 3:00 to 5:00 in the afternoon. The rest of the time was spent relieving throughout the hospital where needed.

It was a good thing I was in the diet kitchen for only one month. I am certainly no cook. My custards either browned too much on top or were not brown enough. My white sauce was lumpy, and when I was told to make 100 grams of coffee, I made a great big pan-full—enough for an army. The first time I made creamed chicken for the soft diets I did not cut the chicken into small enough pieces. I put the diet boxes in the wrong place and the maids carried them to the wrong wards. Then I had to go around through the hospital and hunt them up. I did not send the private patients any olives (I didn't know I should) and I guess every ward must have phoned the D.K. to find out where their olives were, so I had to cart those around to each ward.

One day it was my job to make mayonnaise. The oil had to be added to the rest of the ingredients drop by drop. All went well at first but I thought that would take forever so made the drops bigger and bigger resulting in a soupy mixture. Then I had to begin all over on a new batch and when that was done add the first thin mixture to the good one drop by drop. We had one big batch of mayonnaise when I finished. Another day I had to make rice pudding. The recipe called for eight cups of rice. It did not say cooked or uncooked rice, so I chose uncooked rice. By the time I got through, we had every large pan in the kitchen filled with rice. I think the dietitian thought me hopeless.

After completing my diet kitchen service, I was assigned to day duty in a recovery room to watch a young student nurse who had tried to commit suicide. She was a beautiful girl who one night had overstepped the hospital's strict rules about staying out late. She had not even returned! She was immediately expelled. That hit her so hard that she took a dose of poison and was found unconscious. I was with her a number of days until her parents were able to take her home and I could not leave her unattended for a single moment. In spite of all the stomach lavages, her entire gastrointestinal tract was damaged beyond repair. She would never be the same again, if she lived at all.

In June, Miss Wilkinson, the private room's floor supervisor, went on vacation for three weeks and I was selected to be in charge. Now *she* was a perfectionist and had worked at the Albany Hospital for years. She was so duty struck that she actually hated to take time off. Miss Wilkinson said that every time she came back the place was in a mess, so I was determined that she would not say that this time.

My duties were to pass out all medications, take temperatures, change all dressings, make· rounds with the doctors, do the charts, make out the time schedule, reports, night orders, diet lists, order the supplies, and supervise the serving of trays. My student nurses carried trays, fed patients, gave baths, and made beds. When I returned from my two hours off duty on my first day there, I was told we had a new patient who was a state trooper. His name was Frank Yates. I went to his room to welcome him and my heart flipped! It still does after all these years, whenever I think of him.

This was a busy time as our class was getting ready for graduation. There were formal gowns to buy, white uniforms to have made, photos to be taken, and State Board Exams. Miss Donald was in a quandary. Somehow, because of my Brady Hospital and Tuberculosis (TB) Camp Training, they had forgotten to schedule Materia Medica classes for me at a later date. In order to graduate I had to pass that subject about drugs and other substances used in medicine, their origins, preparation, uses, and effects. I was fit to be tied. I said, "This isn't my fault. Let me take the exam anyway." So I studied the subject on my own, and thank God, I did pass.

Miss Wilkinson returned at the end of three weeks and could not find a single thing to complain about. We had fresh labels on every medicine bottle, new tags on the chart and utility racks, all blankets and linens stacked perfectly, every duty room drawer in order, every ink bottle filled, every pencil sharpened, a full supply of dressings on hand, mirrors and sinks polished, and every room in apple-pie order.

I believe this was the first time I needed to ask my parents for money. They sent me $10.00 a month throughout nurses training and I made do on it. Now I had to have store-bought clothes. I selected a rainbow-hued yellow gold orange chiffon dress for the formal dance and a cocoa brown lace dress for the banquet. My escort for the senior ball was Eugene Galvin, the medical student I dated.

Our banquet was held at the Hampton Hotel and I was class historian. As we were forming in line to enter the dining room, Aunt Gert appeared and I was more than a little embarrassed. She was so proud of me that she had come to hear me read that history! I told her that this was a private gathering and not for the public. She was disappointed but did leave quietly.

Graduation Day was June 10, 1924. The ceremony took place on the lawn where pictures were taken of each of us holding a long-stemmed American Beauty rose.

My family came for the occasion and it was a happy day. A few days later, I was surprised to receive beautiful pearls from Mabel McGowan, my former grade school teacher in Greene. I couldn't imagine when I would wear them, so I gave the necklace to one of my friends. I received other gifts such as handkerchiefs, silk stockings, a silver teaspoon, a gold Eversharp mechanical pencil, an instrument case and $2.00 from each of three people.

\* \* \*

At work, I bubbled all over in telling Frank Yates about these activities and he saw me change from a girl in pink one day to a woman in white the next. He must have been amused when I told him about using rouge on my checks for the three affairs for the first time. Frank just had a way of drawing me out of my shell and was a person I could really talk to, yet I had so little time. Frank gave me a weekend traveling case with my initials on it, which I made much use of in the years to come. I remember being extra particular with his tray and made it most attractive. I brought him books and magazines to read and managed to rub his back and make his bed each day. He had osteomylitis in his leg due to an injury received during a manhunt and was in and out of hospitals for years having the bone scraped and finally his leg amputated.

About this time, Miss Donald called me to her office. I trembled so all the way there that I could hardly speak to her. What had or hadn't I done now? Well, for the first time she was as nice as could be, even smiled, and asked about my plans for the future. I told her that five of us were planning to rent an apartment together after we returned from our month vacation and do private duty. She had other plans. She asked me to be supervisor on the male ward, the most difficult ward in the hospital. "Oh, I couldn't." I said. "I never could do it." "Yes, you can," said she. "Come back and give me your answer in three weeks." I said, "Yes, Miss Donald," and fled, knowing that my answer would still be *no*.

I finished my course of study on August 19, the day before my vacation and went back to her office determined to get this over quickly. She turned around in her chair, smiled and said, "Well? Have you decided?" I said, "Yes, Miss Donald, I've decided ..." but she let me go no farther. She said, "I'm so glad. I know you can take charge there and do it well, and I will help you in any way I can!" And because I was so afraid of her, I did not dare argue.

The girls thought I was crazy. I would be working days for $70 a month and have only two half days off a week. Moreover, they would earn $6 a night and be off as long as they pleased between cases. I know now that this was my destiny and part of the Master's plan. What we think we want, we do not always get and what we are sure we do not want, we are given. We are lumps of clay in God's hands and we get what is best for us.

*My first formal dress*

# Chapter 6

## My Nursing Career Begins
### September 1924—November 1925

> *I asked for a hoe, and I set me to work,*
> *And my red blood danced as I went:*
> *At night I rested, and looking back,*
> *I counted my day well spent.*
> —Eleanor H. Porter

I returned to Albany from my vacation to a furnished house at 568 Park Avenue, not far from the hospital, which Mabel, Nora, Lillian, and Tyl had already rented.

I had two private duty cases prior to assuming my role as supervisor of CT at the beginning of October. One of the cases was a three-year-old girl with pneumonia. She lived in a well-to-do home in the city. I was on twenty-hour duty and slept in a twin bed in her room. I applied mustard plasters to her chest and to her back to stimulate healing. I first made a mixture of dry mustard powder and a small amount of flour mixed with water or egg white to form a paste and spread it onto a cloth that I applied to her chest and back, making sure the mustard paste never came in direct contact with her skin. The girl's mother and grandmother found ways to keep me busy doing things for them in order to earn my money. I felt they had hired me to be a masseuse rather than a nurse and I inwardly resented it.

Once I began working in the hospital, I sent part of my paycheck home each month to pay my parents back for what they had spent for me during the three years of training. I also paid my fifth share of the rent and the "kitty," and lived on the little bit left.

My year of supervising was a breeze and I had full co-operation from Miss Donald and my student nurses. The medical students soon knew where to come for any supplies they needed, for aspirin or cough medicine. One had arthritis in his arms and shoulders and many a rub I gave him with oil of wintergreen before he went to his quarters. One day one of the fellows needed blood to do a sedimentation test, so I offered mine. With a syringe, he drew a little from my left arm but the needle went through the vein causing a subcutaneous hemorrhage that spread over a larger area on the inner side of my arm. He was very concerned about that, but I hadn't known I was a bleeder. It was some time before I could wear short sleeves as it caused too many comments.

One rule that I made for the medical students was that any sterile instruments or syringes they borrowed must be rinsed immediately and left soaking in an emesis basin in the sink. One day I came on duty to find a large unwashed syringe not soaking. That really annoyed me because I tried in every way to help those boys and I expected cooperation from them. Other supervisors would not bother with them and that is why they came to me. I struggled to pull that syringe apart until it broke in my hands taking a chunk of flesh out of my right index finger. Well, I bled all over the place and one of the girls was giving me aromatic spirits of ammonia when in came one of the head medical doctors to make rounds. He sized up the situation and told her to give me a shot of tetanus antitoxin because we did not know whose blood was in that syringe.

At this particular time a Jewish lady whom Tyl was taking care of died. It was a Jewish custom for someone to stay with the corpse around the clock for three days, but lacking enough relatives to stay, the family paid Tyl to act as a substitute. She did not want to go to the mortuary alone, so she asked me to go with her. I knew that if the situation were reversed I would want someone to go with me, so I said yes. This was a new experience for the mortician also, and he felt sorry for us two young girls. He closed the doors between the casket area and where we were to spend the night. Then he gave us magazines to read. That was a long twelve hours. I had to leave before 6 a.m. to get back to my apartment, change, and get on duty by 7 o'clock—with no breakfast.

The second night he gave us a blanket because we had been so cold the night before. About 10 p.m., the undertaker came back downstairs and said he just remembered that the couch opened for a bed. Between the three of us, we got it open, but what a night that was! I slept on the outside, which was on a slant and had to hold on for dear life to keep from falling to the floor.

The third night he propped up my side of the bed. We started out fairly comfortable until I began to itch and develop a temperature. Then I realized that I was having a violent reaction to the tetanus shot that I had been given a few days before.

The year went by very fast. I saw little of the other girls as they had almost continuous private duty night cases. However, each did her own share keeping the house neat and clean. We all washed, starched, and ironed our uniforms, changing at least every two days, so there were always uniforms hanging around the rooms. I spent my evenings alone reading, playing records on the Victrola, and hemstitching. Once the girls had a birthday party for me and gave me a book of poetry by Edgar Guest.

I often went to visit Frank Yates in his hospital room on my time off, as he liked to hear about all my experiences. When he finally left the hospital for his home in Michigan, he came to see me. Frank brought me a bunch of Al Jolson records and a beautiful marquise-cut blue aquamarine ring in a white gold filigree setting. We wrote each other on and off for the next four years but I never saw him again. I lived for his letters and his handwriting was so beautiful. He did not want to get serious because of his worsening leg problem. He said he would never marry and be a burden to anyone. I would have been happy to be his slave and would have followed him around the world barefoot if he had asked me. However, he did not, and he may never have guessed my true feelings about him. Frank became a captain in Barracks K. He had his leg amputated near the hip but the bone infection became steadily worse. I remember receiving a surprise five-pound box of chocolates from him in 1928 when I was working in Monticello. I wrote to him when I went west the following year, telling him all about my experiences. Then his letters stopped and eventually I learned that he had died.

My first year was over and the second had begun on the Critical Trauma Ward. I remember sitting in the nurses dining room one day and looking around at the other supervisors. With but one exception, they were all "old maids" and had started exactly as I had when they finished training. Was this to be my destiny, too? Tyl and I talked it over and decided we would like to try our wings. Lil was engaged to a young newspaper reporter, who was soon to go to Springfield, Massachusetts, so she had plans of her own. Mabel and Nora were older and were content to spend their lives doing private duty and "getting rich quick." However, Tyl and I had great ideas about helping evangelize the world and considered becoming missionaries. We wrote to every service we could think of and soon brochures started pouring in. At first Indian service in the West appealed to us, then Alaska, where we could have immediate appointments in Nome, the farthest point North. We read everything we could find about Alaska and one lone sentence in a book put that idea out of our minds. "Mail delivery was once a month during winter." "Imagine getting thirty newspapers at one time with state news in them!" said Tyl. Our next choice was the Veterans' Administration. There maybe we could do some good. The Army and Navy Nurse Corps would hire young women like us.

Then something occurred that triggered immediate action. Doreen was called on a case in the hospital. Her patient had a friend who was admitted to the same semi-private room. They thought it would be great for her to Special them both and they would share the expense ($3.00 each), but she would have twice the work! That created a great furor. The alumni said this could *not* be done and advised RNs to go on strike, which they did. LPNs and Aides had to be called in. The newspapers made a big issue of this. I decided to resign as soon as the hospital found a replacement for me.

When Gene Galvin decided to intern in a Jersey City hospital for two years, he gave me his fraternity pin, so I was "pinned" because he didn't want to lose me. I could not hurt his feelings by telling him that I was not serious. I thought time would work things out for the best. He visited me in Greene once and met my family and they liked him.

In November 1925, we five girls split up. Mabel and Nora went to New York City along with several other Albany Hospital nurses—all to do private duty there. Nora married and moved to San Francisco, where she became a fur buyer for the City of Paris Department Store. Doreen joined the Henry Street Settlement Nursing Service in New York City as a staff nurse, with the goal of devoting her career to public health nursing.

Tyl and I went to Binghamton where we found an unheated third floor room in a private home with a motherly landlady, and we registered for work. Tyl was called almost at once to care for an elderly lady in a beautiful home full of servants and was with her the entire time she was in Binghamton. I had one short case in a similar home, caring for a lady who owned an exclusive French dress shop. My next assignment was taking care of two young children with diphtheria in the city hospital's isolation building. On my second day with them, I was peppered with a rash and came down with scarlet fever! I had to be put in quarantine for four weeks.

I was not ill too long, so I spent my time playing two-handed pinochle with a ten-year-old boy and helping sick patients. One night, with a sterile surgical gown over my pajamas, I assisted a surgeon with an emergency mastoid operation. When I got out of quarantine, I went home to Greene where Dr. Chapin immediately contacted me to take care of a patient who had just given birth to a premature baby in her home. This was twenty-hour duty and all but one of my uniforms was in Binghamton, so on my four hours off in the evening, I would rush home to wash and iron that uniform before going back on duty.

When I got off that case, I reported to the Binghamton City Hospital that I was ready for work again and they asked me at once to be the night nurse in the isolation building, which had now moved into a three-story house closer to the hospital. That was not what I wanted but I said I would help them out until they found someone if they would pay me private duty wages ($7.00 per a 12-hour shift from 7 p.m. to 7 a.m.) and they agreed. They found no replacement for me for six entire months with not one single night off! I thought they had forgotten me.

I was the only nurse in that building, so I had to run up and down those three flights of stairs constantly. The various disease wards included measles, scarlet fever, diphtheria, mumps, whooping cough, and pneumonia. Most of the patients were children. A basin of Lysol solution and a gown was outside the door to each room. I had to wash my hands and change gowns before and after entering each room. While I was there, half of the children from the orphanage were confined, but there never was a cross infection, for which I was thankful. After the mile walk to my rooming house at seven each morning, I would bathe to get rid of that Lysol smell, then sleep until Tyl got off in the evening.

One night when I came on duty, I found an acquaintance that had just had an emergency appendectomy, complicated by scarlet fever. In the middle of the night, she yelled for me and I found her in a pool of blood, her dressings saturated. "Now don't panic," I said. "This sometimes happens if a stitch breaks. Just keep calm and leave everything to me." I dashed to the phone and called the intern on duty. "I can't come down there," he said. "That isolation building is off limits to me." "Well, I'm here alone and I need someone at once. She's hemorrhaging," I said. He was snippy and vehemently said he would not come. I was furious! Not knowing what else to do, I changed the dressing myself, strapped it tightly and changed her bed, all the while reassuring her everything would be all right. I gave her a drink of warm milk and told her to go to sleep and that I would slip in frequently to check the dressing. "Don't worry, just trust me," I said. And I prayed!

Those six months are a blur. However, I remember the delicious lamb chops the day girls usually left for me to cook in the middle of the night. I never tired of eating lamb chops with fried eggs, bread and butter, and milk.

In July, I collapsed, probably from exhaustion. Tyl found me and was really frightened. The landlady called the doctor and my mother, who came down and stayed with me. She said, "No more of this, young lady. When you get well, we'll take a vacation, maybe to Europe." That was a magic word, "Europe." When I recovered, I did not go back to work. Instead, I went to a travel agency and came home with brochures on European tours. I had earned enough to take us both. Mama and I selected a two-month conducted tour of six countries and in two weeks time we were ready to go. Before we left, Tyl and I sent in our applications to the Veterans' Administration and said we would be available on October 1. I hoped a job would be waiting for me when I returned from Europe.

* * *

On July 24, 1926, Mama and I sailed out of New York Harbor on the S.S. *Minnekahda*. Gene Galvin was at the pier to see me off. The ship carried only tourist third class and if we had had no shore leave at all, the nine-day ocean voyage itself would have been worth the trip. Our privileges were unlimited and advantages far outnumbered any disadvantages. Unrestricted deck space for our promenades, deck sports and contests, and reading or lounging in our steamer chairs contributed as much to our pleasure as the excellent weather all during the trip. My diary gives details of all that we saw in France, Monte Carlo, Italy, and Switzerland. It was a trip to remember and included conducted sightseeing tours, first class hotels, with everything perfectly arranged. At Basel, Switzerland, Mama and I left the tour and went on our own to Germany, Holland, and England. We traveled by train and by boat up the Rhine to Cologne and Bonn where Grandfather Justen was from. When we arrived in Mainz, we took a streetcar to Kessenich to visit Mama's cousin, Rosie Rodins. We spent ten days visiting Rosie, her two sisters, and other relatives and friends whom Mama had seen on her trip there in 1898. Everyone treated us like royalty.

We wanted to visit Amsterdam and London before meeting friends from Greene a week later. Tom, Emma, and Kathleen Bullett had been visiting England so we rode with them to Southampton in their car. We went directly to the pier and watched their automobile be loaded onto the S.S. *Homeric*. This ship was roped off for three classes, so we did not have the freedom we had had on our previous voyage. The weather in September had turned colder and there was quite a bit of rain and rough seas. The second day out people began to get seasick. The dining room and deck were almost empty and since I was not sick, I thought I must be a rugged person. Then on the fourth day, as I was walking on the deck, it suddenly hit me and I had to make a hasty dash to the rail! After that, I was confined to my upper bunk until almost in sight of New York City. Mama weathered it just fine all the way. My recovery was just as sudden as the onset. We arrived in New York on September 21 and drove home to Greene with the Bulletts.

* * *

Upon our return, I found my appointment to the Veteran's Administration Hospital in Perry Point, Maryland, awaiting me. Tyl and I were assigned to the V.A. Mental Hospital and we were to be there within three days. As soon as Tyl arrived on the train from Utica, away we went. I was still in a daze when we reached our destination. We had requested a western facility and never dreamed it would be a mental hospital on the East Coast.

The hospital served 1,000 patients from throughout our nation. The complex was larger than we imagined. There was a gate with a guard at the entrance to the reservation, which was ideally situated on a point extending into Chesapeake Bay. Tyl and I often walked the three-miles around the point each day when we got off night duty at 7 a.m. Wild geese and ducks wintered there. They were a remarkable sight at arrival and take-off times. However, they were noisy, especially in the springtime.

The neuro-psychiatric patients were in separate buildings according to the severity of their condition. Many were in locked buildings whereas others were free to come and go as they pleased. During football season, the fellows on my ward would lie on their beds with their headphones on and listen to the games.

Most of the help in the dining room, nurses' home, mess hall, and grounds were black, so in every way this was a new experience for us as we had worked with very few black people. The nurses' barracks was a two-story building with a long corridor running down the center with an entrance at each end. Midway on the first floor was a large recreation room. Tyl's room was on the second floor, mine on the first across from the bathroom, laundry room, and little kitchen. We did our own laundry in the stationary tubs, scrubbing the clothes on a washboard with yellow laundry soap to remove the stains. Each item needed to be rubbed up and down on the ridges of the washboard before rinsing in water. This was very hard on the arms and fingers and I frequently had raw knuckles. The lines were always full of our clothes and uniforms that we had to starch and iron. Probably we were the only ones who did not send our uniforms to a laundry. One day a nurse jokingly said that she could not decide whether we were the dirtiest or cleanest two that she had ever seen!

Our adventures were many that year. Both of us were twenty-two and full of the zest for life. Mostly the vets we worked with were young, but older than we were. They didn't seem too off-balance to us, so we felt we were angels of mercy sent to help them. They suffered from malaria, epilepsy, shell shock, migraine headaches, etc. Many were in wheelchairs and on crutches and had not recovered from the affects of the wars they had been in. The nerves of some had been so shattered that they had lost the power of speech while others suffered from depression.

According to the patients, the other nurses were all "old battle-axes" from World War I who did not share our sympathetic feelings. However, we just knew how those boys needed girls like us to cheer them up, so we gave up all our evenings to play cards with them at the Red Cross Hut or to attend their dances. We got them more interested in crafts and praised their work.

Some of the fellows on my ward helped me paint all the white iron beds and stands in the ward on my off-duty time. In one month's time, those boys improved noticeably. Hope had come back into their lives and they began to have faith in themselves. We found many to be good singers; some could play musical instruments and one played a saw like a professional. One song that stays in my memory was this:

*"Oh, I wish I had someone to love me,*
*Somebody to call me their own;*
*I would fly to the arms of my darling,*
*And then I would never more roam."*

Another patient wrote poetry. We were continuously amazed at what we drew out of them.

Without us realizing it, some of the fellows began to get a little serious. One hillbilly from North Carolina would not let himself win in a card game. He wanted me to win. Once he could not help winning and he actually shed tears. At Christmas, many of the patients deluged us with lamp-shades, beautifully made leather purses, plants, a manicure set, and fifteen boxes of candy. This was too much. I sent the entire fifteen boxes home "to distribute to the poor," and gradually began to cut down on attending those social evenings.

One rainy day two of the fellows asked Tyl and me to take a ride up the river in a rowboat they had procured and we went. Next day we learned that one of those boys had the worst epileptic seizure he had ever had shortly after he got back. That really brought us to our senses. What if it had happened while we were in that boat—and we had all drowned! I shudder to think of that even now. Our guardian angels were certainly with us!

I remember my first assignment to the mess hall at mealtime to help the attendants watch the patients they had marched from the "locked buildings." This was a new experience for me. Some patients just sat blank and had to be fed, others would swipe food off their neighbor's plate, and others gulped food down practically whole. It was all we could do to keep order. One morning boiled eggs were served for breakfast, and some patients threw them around. I was scooping the egg out of its shell for one man and before I could stop him, he ate the shells just like candy. "Don't try to stop him," yelled the attendant. "He'll knock you down. He's done that for months and it hasn't hurt him yet."

Another Sunday morning, I was sent to a "locked building" to help the attendant there change some eighty beds as it was easier and faster for two to work together. There were a lot of flies in the ward, so I gave one patient a fly swatter and showed him how to swat flies on the wall. When we finished our work that patient was in the same spot with the swatter still in his hand waiting for the first fly to come back. The attendant thanked me for helping him and said, "You didn't act as if you heard a single thing those patients said while we were working." "I didn't," I said. "They weren't talking to me." "But they were saying the worst kind of foul language, which is all their minds run to," he said. However, I actually had not heard *one* word; I was intent on my work and seeing that none came close to me. I never saw a case history on those patients as those files were kept under lock and key. It seemed incredible that there were so many psychotic patients who were once the pride of our Army. I asked one of the doctors about this. "Why?" "It wasn't the war," he answered, "but the syphilis that nearly ninety percent of our patients contracted during the war." [4]

One of my patients was in charge of the linen room and patients' personal clothing, and he was a perfectionist. Everything was folded and stacked just so and each cubbyhole neatly labeled with a patient's name. No one had ever heard him utter a single word. I tried and tried to get him to say yes or no, but he would only nod or shake his head, and would not even try to form a word. One day an attendant went in that room to get something for a patient and he left the cupboard in disarray. The fellow in charge came in and was livid. He beat up the attendant and pitched him out the door, all without saying a word.

Tyl and I worked five days a week so made the most of free weekends. Our first outing was to Philadelphia to see places of historical interest. After getting off the train, we hopped on a streetcar and took seats in the rear section. A

---

[4] The first real cure for syphilis was found in the 1940s with the discovery of penicillin.

black man entering at the same time said to us, "You'd better go up front." We said, "Oh, this is all right." He said, "But this is the colored section." I said, "Oh, we don't mind." He acted uneasy but did not know what to say next. Then someone behind us whispered, "We are not supposed to sit with whites." Well! We were thunderstruck, but we did move. We had not known about segregation before but our eyes were certainly aware of it after that.

On other weekends, we visited Valley Forge, Baltimore, and Washington. My parents came on a trip to Washington and we went sightseeing with them. Later, Tyl's two sisters drove down to visit and the four of us went to Washington for a couple days. This time we stayed at a YWCA dormitory. In the middle of the night, a bat flew in the open window and everyone screamed. When we finally settled down, each one of us spent the rest of the night with our heads underneath the sheet.

In the spring, a new bridge was being built across the Susquehanna River between Perryville and Havre de Grace, Maryland, and construction workers were needed. Tyl wrote to her young brother Emil, and suggested he come down and apply for a job. In no time at all, he came and was hired at once. Emil found a room to rent over a restaurant, but every time he came to see us, he smelled like fried food. Therefore, Tyl had him take a bath in the bathroom across the hall from my room. It was her idea that he sleep in my room as it was next to the outside door and he could leave early before anyone was up, so I slept upstairs with her. No one ever knew about this, so well did she arrange the timing for everything.

Tyl was in charge of a TB ward at this time and told me about one of her young bedridden patients who had been unresponsive since his admission. She would not believe that he was deaf or blind and endeavored to draw him out of himself. On my way off duty, I would stop for her and we would sit beside his bed and talk to him just as if he understood. The day finally came when he made eye contact with us and we were ecstatic. Then followed a long slow series of little miracles: from the day his eyes followed us, to the days he could say his first name, hold a spoon, sit up, feed himself, and finally to be lifted into a wheelchair. Where there is life, there is hope, we believed.

Tyl's father decided he wanted to take a trip back to the Old Country (Germany) and he wanted her to go with him. Therefore, she resigned and left on May 1, 1927. I hated to see her go and things were different after that. I did more crocheting and embroidering, went out less, and no longer went to the Red Cross Hut. Emil found a different place to room and finally went home.

Gene Galvin came down to see me once and somehow there was little to talk about. We had grown apart. As I stood on the depot platform watching his train go north out of sight, I had a fleeting feeling that it was carrying him away from me forever.

\* \* \*

In September, fate stepped into my life in the form of a phone call from Katherine English saying that her daughter Mary had been in an automobile accident and was in serious condition in a hospital in Monticello, New York. She wanted me to come up and take care of my younger cousin. I said I could not leave on a minute's notice and my vacation was not due. Katherine was hysterical. She would not believe that strangers could take good care of Mary. So, I agreed to talk with my chief nurse who said if I wanted to leave, I could give two weeks notice. When I phoned Katherine back, she said, "Okay, come then." Therefore, I wrote the superintendent of the Monticello Hospital and asked if there would be a chance for employment there. She replied saying they had an opening for night nurse.

I left Perry Point on October 1, traveling by train to New York City where I changed trains to the O & W Railroad to Monticello. I shall never forget that spectacular ride through the Catskills in the caboose of the train with only trainmen on it. There was no passenger car as tourist season was over and the death knell of that line had sounded with its end not far off. The fall foliage colors were at their best and the scenery breathtaking. I had never seen a grander sight. When I arrived at the Monticello Hospital, I learned that Mary was better and would be leaving the next day, but that I could go on duty 11 to 7 that night. You can imagine how tired I was the next morning.

When the month was over, the superintendent asked me to be the day supervisor of the whole hospital for $100 a month and I accepted. This was the most I had ever been paid. The hospital was a Jewish hospital and strictly kosher so was quite an experience for me. The nurses laughed at me in the dining room when they saw me salt my food. "Oh, you'll get used to this just like we did," they said, but I did not believe it.

After working for nearly four months, I took a bus home for a weekend, as it was my parents wedding anniversary. They met me at the bus station in Binghamton. On the way to Greene, Mama asked if I would like anything special to eat while I was home. I said "Ham." However, when I tasted it, I said, "My! How salty this is!" Mama said she had freshened it especially for me, as she knew kosher food and thought it wise to soak the ham in water to remove some of the salt before cooking.

When I returned to Monticello, people inundated me with questions about an article in the local newspaper. I did not know what they were talking about until Mama sent me a clipping from the *Chenango American,* which had been copied from the *Monticello Times.* This is it in part: "The resemblance of Mildred English to Frances St. John Smith, the missing college girl, caused the Park Restaurant proprietor a wild ride to Middletown and the loss of the $15,000 reward. She was not the missing girl. Miss English made a trip to the city last week, leaving on the Middletown bus at 6:30 in the morning. Before taking the bus, she went into the Park Restaurant to have breakfast. Some time after she had gone, the waiter remarked to the owner that she bore a strong resemblance to the missing college girl. Both rushed to his car and in a jiffy were off to Middletown driving as fast as he could. They arrived at the bus depot in Middletown just the bus pulled in, and as the young nurse stepped to the station platform. They both seized her, crying 'Miss Smith, Miss Smith, Frances, Frances! Please be yourself!' But Miss English simply couldn't see it that way, and with the aid of three policemen, the bus driver, an Erie conductor, and a long-distance call to the superintendent of the Monticello Hospital finally convinced Mr. Karamechedis and the waiter that she was not Miss Smith, the missing college girl." I knew nothing about the girl being missing and had not been aware of anyone calling to me.

One evening that winter the nurses at the Liberty Hospital invited the Monticello Hospital nurses to their town for supper. As we sat around the long table getting acquainted with each other, a nurse across the table from me mentioned that she had recently come to Liberty from the Jersey City Hospital, so I asked if she knew Gene Galvin there. "Oh, yes," she said. "He just married one of the nurses there." Well! Was that ever a shock! I pulled myself together and somehow got through the evening. The next day I boxed up Gal's fraternity pin and mailed it to him with the briefest of notes. "Congratulations! But why didn't you tell me?" Suddenly a great weight was lifted from my heart and I felt like a leaf blowing through the air. Free! Free! Free At Last was all I could think. Then I realized what I had vaguely felt all along, that he wasn't the one for me. He answered by return mail, something about his surprise and what did I mean? I tore the letter up and that was the end.

In April, I went down to New York City to see Mabel, Nora, and Tyl, who was now living with them in a nice apartment on Park Avenue. Lil had married and had moved to Massachusetts. They wanted me to come and join them. "It could be just like the old days." No, it couldn't—not for me. They had become so worldly, so self-centered, so money and clothes conscious. I was still an idealist and wanted more out of life. Their life was not for me. I wanted to see the world, go where the wind would take me. Therefore, I went to a travel agency and stocked up on brochures.

About this time, the superintendent of the Monticello Hospital retired and her replacement was not easy to work for. My duties as supervisor had nothing to do with her as business manager, but she kept forgetting that she was no longer nursing. She started in at mealtime watching me serve trays. "Now just a little more of this on ..." and "not so much of that," etc., etc. (I knew the patients' preferences, not she.) I put up with that for every tray for three days, getting more irked by the minute. Finally, I handed her the serving spoon and said, "Here, you do it. This kitchen doesn't need two of us." And I walked out. Well, she ran right after me, full of apologies. She actually had not realized that she was not talking to a probationer. "Please come back," she said. "Please!" I said, "Only on one condition." She knew what I meant and never bothered me again.

I wrote home and said I was thinking about going to the West Coast and wanted to see everything on the way, in essence, to work my way across the country. My younger brother Paul had left for Chicago a year earlier and was now working in San Francisco. His letters prompted me to want to see the country as well. The summer season in the Catskills would start Memorial Day. From then until Labor Day, the resorts would be flooded with wealthy Jews from New York City. That was always a busy "and profitable" time for nurses, so I wanted to get away from there before the stampede, as it would be next to impossible to resign then.

Mama told her friend Mrs. O'Leary about my plans. She said her daughter Irene would be finishing training at St. Joseph's Hospital in Syracuse in June and that Irene wanted to visit her three sisters and a brother who lived throughout the West. The two mothers thought it would be great if we girls went together. Although we were both Greene High School graduates, we only knew each other by sight. So, I immediately wrote to Irene telling her about my planned itinerary. She replied that it sounded good to her if we could fit in visits to her family, which was not hard to do.

I left Monticello on June 1 to spend a couple weeks preparing for my trip. Shortly after arriving home, I accompanied my parents and the O'Learys to Celia O'Leary's graduation from Syracuse University, then to St. Joseph's Hospital to talk with Irene. The result was that Irene, Celia, and I decided to see the West together!

# Chapter 7

## Westward Bound

*Two roads diverged in a wood, and I--*
*I took the one less traveled by,*
*And that has made all the difference.*
—Robert Frost

Irene, Celia, and I left by train from Binghamton on the morning of June 18, 1928. The first stop was Buffalo where we made connections for Niagara Falls. It rained all the time we were at the Falls, so we did not walk around but instead we took the gorge trip and it only cost $1.50 for the round trip. When the trolley had nearly completed the trip, we stopped off to go through the Niagara Power Company plant. It contained the largest hydroelectric generators ever built at that time, and took only seven men to run the plant. After the twenty-five-mile ride back to Buffalo, we left for Chicago on the 9:15 evening train, and slept most of the night. It was still raining when we arrived, so we took the first train out— the Colorado Limited to Denver. It was a much nicer train than any Eastern train on which I had ridden, the seats on the coaches being separate and having a footrest and lever to raise or lower the back.

As the train crossed Illinois, the farms seemed to be large and prosperous-looking. There were acres of foot-high corn in perfectly even rows and lots of trees, which were almost absent when we traveled across Nebraska. The cornfields of the Midwest thrilled us farm girls. In Nebraska, the farmers were haying. Colorado was entirely different and the scenery changed as soon as we reached the state line. At first, there were rolling hills and later on large ranches with cattle and horses grazing in the fields. The roads all looked like good ones—improved but not macadam or cement as in the East.

When we approached Denver, the snow-capped mountains in the distance made us impatient to reach our destination for it had been a long and tiresome journey. After making a few inquiries once we arrived in Denver, we bought all-expense tickets to tour the Rocky Mountain National Park for three days. The cost was $39 each. It seemed good to get into a car again and an open one at that. It was a pleasant ride through the city and foothills of the Rockies with their little villages until we finally reached the mountains. After arriving at Estes Park Village, another motorcar drove us four miles up the mountain to the lovely chalets.

We loved every minute there and were up at 4 a.m. to see the sunrise and to take a long walk around a heart-shaped lake before breakfast. At 9 a.m., a young man saddled horses for us to take a guided horseback ride up into the mountains. The fellow who took care of the forty horses was a real honest-to-goodness cowboy and had been all his life. He went with our party in the morning, as we were unused to horses. At first, I was very frightened in the saddle, but soon got over it. When we reached the end of the trail, we tied the horses and finished the rest of the way on foot over jagged and precipitous rocks. When we got to the top, we saw the most beautiful panoramic view of the mountains that equaled any of the Alps in Switzerland.

In the afternoon, we took an unguided twenty-one-mile horseback trip in another direction. We were so tired and hungry when we got back that we could hardly get off our horses. The next morning we left the chalets and continued by bus through the park. I intended to count the sharp hairpin curves as we traveled up the side of the mountains, but lost count. Four were so sharp that it was necessary for the driver to back up the bus before making the turn. When we were well above the tree line, the vegetation grew scarce and a bitterly cold wind blew something fierce. Three days before a heavy snowstorm blocked sections of the road and a crew of 150 men worked to clear it so buses could get through. At one place, the men had dug through twenty-three-foot snowdrifts for quite some distance. I wanted to get a snapshot of it because I thought no one would ever believe it if I told them, but the driver had to go fast so as not to get stuck in the ruts. The highest point we reached was 11,797 feet, but the altitude did not affect us at all. We went up those mountains in low speed and came down in second gear. The distance from the chalets to the lodge, where we stayed that night, was only thirty-nine miles. At the top of the mountain we were wrapped in heavy blankets up to our chin, and at the foot of the mountain we didn't even need a sweater.

Eleven miles from our destination, the road was under repair and being scraped, thus leaving a ridge of dirt and stones in the center. The driver drove astride the ridge. When he struck a level space, he picked up speed. Suddenly there was a crash; the crankshaft had struck a stone damaging the oil tank and all the oil drained out. Fortunately, an emergency station with a phone was not too far distant, so the driver went to phone for help. While waiting for the relief bus, we enjoyed walking around, never realizing our faces were getting sunburned. Finally, the bus arrived and towed us the remaining eleven miles. We were a sight when we reached the lodge, bespattered with dirty snow and dust and sunburned. After cleaning up, we took a six-mile walk. In the evening, we rode down to the chalets with other young folks to attend a dance and forgot all about the mishap during the day.

The next day, on the 240-mile trip back to Denver, we stopped at the Argo gold mine and mill, the largest mill of its type in the world, and at Lookout Mountain to see Buffalo Bill's grave. We went to a YWCA where we spent the evening getting cleaned up. While my hair dried, I wrote much of what you read here to the folks at home. Suddenly, a knock came on our door. Miss O'Leary was wanted on the phone. We panicked for a moment until we learned it was a girlfriend of Celia's who lived a few miles outside the city. She had just received a letter from Greene saying we would be staying at the YWCA. Well, she and her husband came right over to see us and took us back to their home. The next morning, which was Sunday, they brought us back to early Mass at the cathedral and to the railroad station in time to catch the 8:15 train to Salt Lake City. What a spectacular ride it was through the Rockies! The train stopped for ten minutes at the Royal Gorge to let the passengers see the Hanging Bridge, the 3,000-foot perpendicular walls, and view the thirty-foot width of the gorge. It was a most impressive view!

After arriving at our hotel in Salt Lake City, a hotel bus immediately took us to the Mormon Tabernacle where an organ recital was given each noon for the benefit of visitors. That afternoon, we took a sixty-mile Gray Line Tour to the Bingham Canyon Mine, one of the world's largest open-pit copper mines. It opened the year I was born and is estimated that it will take more than sixty-nine years for it to be worked.[5] The next morning, we took a second Grays Tour throughout the city and into the country, following the trail taken by Brigham Young and his pioneer followers in 1847. We liked Salt Lake City nearly as well as we did Denver, only it was dreadfully hot.

At noon, we caught the train to Idaho Falls where Mr. and Mrs. Hersley met us at the station when we arrived at 8:15 that evening of June 26. Stasia Hersley, the girls' older sister, drove us to their home, six miles from the city, where we spent a whole month.

The first thing we did was change into comfortable clothes. Stasia had hurried to get their newly built house ship-shape for us, even to painting the kitchen chairs white. I put on my black satin kimono, which I had spent hours making, lining it with yellow satin and embroidering a large peacock on the back. I was very proud of it. We sat on those white chairs in the scorching heat and related all of our experiences to date. When I got up I was stuck fast, and my beautiful kimono was a mess!

That first night we three girls slept in the Hersley's bed and sweltered and they slept in their unfinished attic. That was enough for us. The rest of the month, we slept outside

---

[5] The Bingham Canyon Mine is still in operation, and is the second largest copper mine in the world. It can be seen from outer space.

on the ground with a blanket under us. What a wonderful experience to watch the stars move across the sky all night in that very flat country. One night, two horses broke through a fence and nibbled at our toes, giving us quite a fright.

The Fourth of July was a day to remember. Irene asked George Hersley to cut off her long straight red hair, even insisting on a boyish cut. It was just too hot to bother with hairpins. The next day, I asked him to cut mine too, but I wanted a feminine bob as I had had a fresh permanent before I left home. We never went back to long hair again.

Two young fellows in the neighborhood became frequent callers. They took us to the Fourth of July celebration, to Heise Hot Springs where we swam in the naturally heated pool, and to a dance. One all-day trip to the Annual Indian Sun Dance was unforgettable. We sat on the ground among the squaws and their papooses while the men danced the hours away to see which one would hold out longest and become the new chief. The boys' old car had five flat tires on that trip, to their chagrin, but to us each got funnier until we were all hysterical.

One day a young friend of the Hersleys was taken to the hospital and we two nurses were asked to special her. Irene took the day shift so I went to relieve her at 7 p.m. We had our uniforms with us as we eventually planned to work. The patient was dying so Irene said she would stay with me, as it would not be long. And it wasn't. While I removed the intravenous and prepared her for the morgue, Irene cut the woman's fingernails. Three days later, we attended the funeral and when we looked at the body in the casket, we gasped! Those fingernails were fully an inch long! We had never seen anything like that before, nor since. At the grave, I wept right along with the family. "Why are you crying?" asked Irene. "You don't know her." I cried for the loved ones left behind.

Farming in this area was different from back home. Stasia's husband irrigated his sugar beet fields, which was an interesting and somewhat complicated process. Haying time was busy on the farm so we had not planned to stay long. However, George and Stasia insisted that we stay until it was finished and a five-acre sugar beet field was weeded. Then they would take us to Yellowstone Park, as they wanted to see it, too. So Irene and I offered to help do that weeding. Celia was the smart one and helped Stasia with the housework and meals. We were up every day at daybreak and out in the field with our hoes until noon. We were nearly half done only to find that the weeds were now as thick as when we had started. Those sweet clover roots must have gone halfway to China. It was a hopeless task! George said his men could finish it after the haying was done.

We joyfully watched the men unload the final wagon, by hayfork, onto the last of his haystacks. The men dared us to let them hoist us up on the huge stack for a look around. Going up was easy and the view from there was like being on a mesa, but I was afraid to come down from such a height. Finally, one of the men had to go up for me and hold me with one arm while he held on to the fork with his other hand as we swung down together. I had gripped that fork so tightly that I could hardly open my hands when we reached bottom. *Never again* will I do that!

The five of us left for a week in Yellowstone Park on July 26. We were in khaki shirts, trousers, and hats, and Irene and I in our hobnail-soled hiking hoots. George removed the covers from the trunk of the coupe and there the two of us sat on a bench. We could just see over the top of the car and when it rained, we held an umbrella over us. Everyone who passed us turned to look and we rather enjoyed being the center of attention. A collapsible metal rack held our canvas-covered luggage on the running board and the tent and bedrolls were strapped on the bumper.

At Yellowstone Lake, George and Stasia met friends who were camping there. They took us for a motorboat ride and we trolled for trout, but only I was lucky enough to catch one. We had a wonderful time camping that week and marveled at God's wondrous works. We drove to Cody, Wyoming, then to the park's north entrance at Gardiner and finally to Livingston, Montana, where Irene and I took our leave of the other three and resumed our trip by railroad to Glacier National Park in northern Montana.

Arriving at the park entrance, we checked our luggage and hiked twelve miles that afternoon to the first shelter, carrying our canvas shoulder bags, sweaters, and Irene's umbrella "for protection." The next day we walked eighteen miles over a rugged trail through breathtaking mountain scenery and were so tired that we barely made it to the shelter. The third day we had such "charley horses" that we could hardly get out of bed, so we were forced to change our plans somewhat. We took the steamer across the lake there to the next shelter and rented horses for an eight-day spectacular trail trip with others, through the park, and back to Glacier Park Headquarters. It was an experience of a lifetime.

Celia had gone to Chinook, Montana, to visit her sister, Loretta, who was superintendent of schools there, so that became our next stop. Loretta was shocked to see us weather-beaten and so brown. She immediately started to bleach us out and curl our hair before showing us off to her friends. (In those days, having a tan indicated a life of outdoor labor and was not looked on with favor in society.) On August 20, Loretta took the three of us in her little car 500 miles north to Lloydminster, Saskatchewan, to visit their brother, Tom O'Leary, and family who were home-steading there. This trip along the Meridian Road between Alberta and Saskatchewan was a memorable one. Although it was flat, treeless prairie land, it was interesting. North of the U.S. border, all was wilderness, just gently waving flatland with nothing in sight but the great canopy of sky over us. It was eerie—like being alone on top of the world—and I do not remember seeing another car.

Suddenly, on the right side of the road, there was an enormous flock of sheep everywhere, and only one man with them and not a house as far as the eye could see. She stopped the car and we just looked, and looked. I had to have a picture of those sheep. I walked a long way across the terrain before the sheepherder noticed me, and then held up my camera to show him that I wanted him in the picture. He understood but told me to wait and he would call the sheep closer. "I'll tell you when to take it," he called.

He stood perfectly still and called to the sheep. They stopped grazing and every head raised and looked toward him. He called again and immediately they started running toward him. The dog got excited and knew it was his duty to round up the stragglers and away he went to do his job. Such perfect obedience! All ran toward their shepherd, around and around him, tightening the huge circle. Again, he said something to the flock and at once, all was quiet, then he straightened up tall in the center, from which he had not moved a foot, raised his crook beside him and called to me, "All steady now." I shall never forget the sight. I wish I had talked with him and learned about his life with the sheep and with God. How did those sheep keep from crushing him? Perhaps he kept them at arm's length from him with that staff which, I learned later, is used to extricate a lamb from a pit or thorn bush or from the clutches of a predator. A shepherd leads his sheep; he does not drive them and they know and trust only him. When he lowered his crook, they started moving away again.

On this trip, we passed an isolated Russian church and a lovely cemetery with fancy iron crosses, a large oat field where the grain reached our armpits, then miles and miles of golden wheat fields on each side of the unfenced one-track road, and finally the O'Leary homestead and the young wife's beautiful English garden. On September 2, Irene and I left Chinook for Alameda (twenty miles north of the North Dakota border) to visit more of her sisters. Since Celia had no teaching job in view back East, Loretta persuaded her to stay and teach in a rural school near Turner, Montana, with three other teachers.

Will and Mary Shepherd met us at the Alameda Station and drove us the six miles to their log house on a large wheat ranch. Harvesting season had begun, so Will, his two young nephews from England, and a neighbor were cutting the wheat. We helped Mary and the hired girl, Mabel, get ready for the fifteen threshers who would soon appear. The bunkhouse needed cleaning, the single beds had to be made, and some new pillows needed to be made from feathers that Mary had been saving. Later, we learned that one of the men felt a mouse inside his pillow in the middle of the night and furiously hurled the pillow across the room.

Suddenly Mary became ill with acute appendicitis. Will rushed her to the hospital and Irene went along to take care of her. Mary was a frail, red-haired woman with an artificial limb and her recovery took much longer than expected. To make matters worse, the hired girl's parents had already started threshing on their farm and Mabel was needed at home. Will and I drove for miles around the country looking for a girl to take her place but not one was found. So, Mabel instructed me on how to do the daily chores and even had fifteen pie crusts made ahead when she left.

On Saturday night Will, Nelson, Edmond, and I went to town and since each of us had various errands to do, we separated. When I finished I went directly to the car and sat in the backseat a whole hour before any of the others came. I saw the boys pass by twice acting as if they were looking for someone. The third time, I called and asked them where everyone was. Nelson said, "What are you doing in that car?" I said, "Waiting for the rest of you." "But this is a Pontiac," he said. "Sure, I know it," I said. "But ours is an Oldsmobile," he insisted. They had looked everywhere for me and the owner had waited in the garage a whole hour for me to get out of his car, so he could go home. I never lived that down.

The threshers arrived two days before Mary came home and she was confined to her bed upstairs the entire three weeks the men were there. Irene and I took over Mabel and Mary's duties. I was so glad to have had the experience of working with Mabel first and was able to plan the daily routine, which included feeding the workers four times a day. The meals had to be hearty and ready on time. We used some of the cans of preserves and canned vegetables and fruits stored in the cellar.

Will had the wood fire going in the range for us every morning when we got up at 5 a.m. to get breakfast for the crew. Breakfast consisted of hot porridge, thick bacon slices, boiled eggs, freshly baked bread, jam, butter, and strong coffee. Mabel said they always had the same thing. Dinner was at 11 a.m. The first day we served a 9 lb. roast, boiled potatoes, string beans, and pie. We had expected to have enough meat and potatoes left over to make hash for supper, but they ate every scrap of food. We soon learned to prepare huge platters of hot roast beef or pork, large bowls heaped with mashed potatoes, turnips, carrots, and other vegetables and large containers of gravy, plus two slices of pie for most men. In the mid-afternoon, Irene and I drove the pick-up truck to the field with a huge pot of coffee and a supply of sandwiches, cookies, tarts, or doughnuts for the workers. The evening meal was about 7 p.m.

As soon as the breakfast work was over, we would make up the beds in the bunkhouse, changing them if necessary, and do the washing. The old Maytag washer was connected by a belt to a motor in a back room and what troubles we had with that! The fine black soil in that country sure made clothes and those forty-five-plus towels dirtier than I had ever believed possible. Moreover, the soapsuds in that hard well water always left a scum, so we had to rinse and re-rinse everything, but all were a joy to behold once we hung them to dry on clotheslines in the breeze.

Our next chore was separating the milk and churning butter from the six cows that Nelson and Edwin milked first thing in the morning. The boys always left plenty of split wood for the stove on hand for us. In the afternoon when all the cleaning and baking was done, Irene and I heated water and carried it up to our little room where we took turns taking sponge baths. Each bedroom had a pitcher and washbowl set as there was no bathroom in the house.

In the late afternoon, it became my job to ride the little horse named Fly out to the pastures and bring the cows in for milking. We were busy every minute and our muscles became hard as iron from carrying all those buckets of water from the well to the house each day for all our needs.

Once I suggested we change the menu by having fried eggs for a change. However, that was a disaster. Thirty eggs just did not cook fast enough and the men were leaving the table before the last eggs were done! Then I thought soup would be a change so we saved all the beef bones and vegetable waters, added celery and onions and whatever we had. The men loved it and said they had never had that before at any place they had worked. Irene's piecrusts were not like Mabel's but the men did not complain. My first cake was a chocolate layer. The recipe read nine teaspoons of baking soda. I thought that was a lot but put it in anyway. Then the cooked chocolate icing was too hard to spread and looked so unattractive that I covered it with a white frosting. Once again, no one complained. I think the men liked us rather than just putting up with us.

The threshing crew traveled from farm to farm with huge machines that would "thresh" the wheat and oats, separating the grain from the straw. The men made their way up from the south every year, working on the same farms and ending up in Canada. Actual threshing was continuous from September 18 to October 11. I do not think I ever worked as hard in my life as I did the first six weeks that we were in Alameda. Once it was over, everyone relaxed. We women went to a quilting party and all of us went to every country school dance for miles around and stayed until 5 a.m. The men began plowing in the fields using six-horse teams and transporting the wheat to large grain elevators. Huge straw stacks could be seen everywhere. It was a busy, interesting, rewarding life.

One day a distant neighbor asked if one of us would call on his young wife who was ill. I volunteered and rode horseback for miles over back roads to see what I could do. I loved riding that horse and sang all the time. I felt God was so close to me. It seemed that He was everywhere in that level vastness. The girl was in bed in a wind-swept shack, her two-year-old son playing with toys on the floor. She had had a miscarriage and there was no fire, no food, and no clean clothes in the house. I built a fire in the kitchen range and put large pans of water on to heat, dressed the boy, cleaned up the place, gave her a bath, washed all the clothes by hand and hung them on the lines to dry, then cooked some potatoes, the only food that I found. When I got back to the Shepards, I told the husband that his wife was all right but just needed food. Mary sent some home with the husband.

One night Nelson and Edwin went to a dance with their own girlfriends so we played tricks on them. We sewed up the bottoms of their pajama legs and the cuffs of their sleeves and folded the top sheets on their beds so they could only get halfway in. Then we set tin cans on each step of the stairs with a string between them and the inside doorknob of the door at the foot of the stairs. When the boys returned home and opened the door, down tumbled all the cans. We rolled in hysterics when we heard the crash and their reaction to later discoveries.

We went to visit Fred and Veronica Coffey for a few days. She was another sister of Irene's. While the girls visited, I went duck hunting with Fred and his dog to a nearby slough. He shot fifteen beautiful mallard ducks in no time and that night his threshers plucked them in their bunkhouse. Boy! There were feathers everywhere! At one meal, we had all those livers and gizzards and hearts. I thought that for once I would have all I wanted. However, in the middle of the night in my attic room I sure was sick and filled the white washbowl and even the thunder mug under the bed. I have never cared for wild game since that unfortunate experience.

Early in November, Irene's two sisters and husbands took us up to Minot, North Dakota, to Aunt Molly's where we roomed and boarded for the next three months. Our funds were running low so we planned to work in Minot just long enough to earn enough money to take us to the coast.

After registering at the local Lutheran Hospital, I was called on a case almost at once. My first assignment was 100 miles away in Fessenden, North Dakota, to care for a pneumonia patient in his home. I was on twenty-four-hour duty for eleven days and earned $66. Back in Minot, the hospital called me for a five-day case, then one for four days, and Irene sat idle at home. We could not understand why the hospital did not call her. My next case was fifty miles north of the border for thirteen days. I got the flu while I was there and was sicker than my patient was, but I managed to take care of her even though I was unable to swallow water, which just came back through my nose. Irene went to Alameda for the holidays, so phoned me to come up there when I finished my job. I went up there on January 2, but found everyone was ill. I simply could not stand the -48° temperature so returned to Minot two days later.

Here it was, January 1929, and I was still in North Dakota. I had been gone from home for more than six months. My first case of the year was taking care of a Christian Science patient. This was a new experience for me. The doctor told me to do the best I could for her but she refused all medications and depended solely on her Christian Science Healer, who was in and out frequently. However, in time the Healer became exasperated and told me not to call her so much. Therefore, I told my patient that the Healer was too busy to come but was praying for her at home. I tried to get my patient's mind off herself, to do her own praying, and that God worked through doctors, all to no avail.

Toward the end of January, the superintendent of nurses called me to her office and offered me the position of assistant night supervisor. I said that our plans were to leave for Oregon just as soon as I got off my case. She pleaded with me to take the position for at least the rest of the winter, so I finally agreed. Perhaps this was my destiny. She told me to sign the contract on my way off duty. As she pushed the contract across the desk, she said, "Oh, by the way, I didn't get your religion." "I'm Catholic," I answered. I will never forget her expression as she pulled the contract back. "Oh, I'm so sorry," she said, "but it is the policy of this hospital not to have Catholics on our staff." Then it hit me. Irene's name was O'Leary while mine was English. Of course, they would expect her to be Catholic, but not me. That was the real reason she got so little work, even though the superintendent now assured me that it was okay to do private duty there. I thought to myself, "Don't people know what being a Christian means?" When I told Irene, she agreed that the sooner we left North Dakota the better.

So, on February 3, we left for Salem, Oregon, stopping at Chinook, Montana, en route where Loretta took us up to Turner, Montana, to see Celia in her schoolhouse apartment. Three other teachers shared the apartment but were gone the night we were there. The four of us slept together in Celia's bed and every time one turned, the other had to turn also. We tucked our underwear under the covers at the foot of the bed to be warm in the morning.

\* \* \*

In Salem, we had no trouble finding a room for rent. We immediately registered at the Central Registry and both of us were soon called on private duty cases at the hospital.

This was all twenty-hour duty, so Irene and I were only together on our four-hour break, which we spent washing clothes or dry cleaning (with naphtha gas), taking baths, shampooing our hair, and writing home. It was great to be working again and having an income. When the end· of March came, we both finished our cases at the same time so we immediately packed a suitcase and took off for San Francisco for Easter to visit my brother, Paul. As we were anxious to see the city, we three took Gray Lines tours to all the places of interest and had a great time. We even tried out secondhand cars, which we thought about buying. Not seeing what we wanted, we asked Paul to keep on the lookout for a good one to buy for us, and drive it up to Salem on his vacation.

We left to return to Salem and because it was such a beautiful April day, we decided to send our suitcases on and hike back the Redwood Highway from Sausalito. Paul thought it was a crazy notion and was not in favor it. He said we were expecting too much thinking we could catch rides in automobiles for 600 miles. We got several short rides and then a really long one to Eureka. I was carsick much of the way but perked up when we reached the coast. The driver took us to a hotel on the north side of the city but warned us to be careful because the town was full of lumbermen.

Irene and I ate at a nearby Italian restaurant and all the men stared at us. A beautiful Hawaiian waitress, whose traveling show had been stranded there, said more waitresses were needed and the owner offered us jobs. She said we could even room upstairs with her, but we were not interested. Back at the hotel, every man there also stared at us, so the minute we got in our room, we barricaded the door with the dresser and slept with our clothes on.

There were no rides as we went north from Crescent City and our thin summer coats and strap-on patent leather slippers were not adequate for the weather. It was out of season and nothing was open along that road. About suppertime, we stopped at a truck stop for hot food. Irene accidently left her gloves behind when we left, so I let her wear one of mine and every now and then, we would switch gloves. It began to rain, then sleet, and night was approaching. We wondered what to do and really prayed. Then along came a big empty lumber truck. We stood and just looked at it as it passed. "No Riders" was on the windshield. Suddenly the truck stopped, backed up, and the driver asked if we would like a ride. "Oh, yes," we said in unison. I sat next to the window and shivered, my chest aching and I thought, "I'm getting pneumonia." We did not notice another habitation during that ride and the driver could not understand why we were way out there in the wilds. We told him we were on our way to Salem, but nothing else. A small briefcase containing combs, toothbrushes, and our nighties was our only luggage. We were too exhausted to talk, so he did not learn much from us. He said he would take us to the depot at Grants Pass where we could take the midnight train north, which was fine with us. Then he told us about a box factory there that employed women and were always hiring more workers. He kept bringing up that subject, wages, and he even drove around that factory when we got there. At the depot, he found the station agent and told him to build a fire in the stove to dry us out while we waited a couple of hours for the train.

Once on the train, we immediately lay down on our seats with our purses under our heads for a pillow and fell asleep. Twice some man, who said there was a sleeping car, aroused me and said I could have his bunk. The same man approached Irene. Everyone tried to be kind, but got nowhere with us.

We arrived in Salem the next morning; gray skies were overhead and snow covered the ground. We had quite a long way to walk to our rooming house and our clothes were a wrinkled mess. We wasted no time in heading for bed. And then, did we ever sleep! Surprisingly, neither of us caught a cold on that arduous 600 miles adventure. The Lord had certainly watched over us on that trip. We decided we would never be that foolish again.

In June, Paul found just the car for us, for $200. He was true to his word and drove it up from San Francisco. It was a used *STAR* with pinwheel fans on the radiator and fenders and we loved it at first sight. The previous owner called it "Little Firefly," so we did too. We had bought a tent, blankets, and camping equipment and were waiting when Paul arrived. Our gear filled up the backseat when we were all loaded with just enough room for one of us. Before leaving Salem, we had the car checked in a Star garage to be sure that it was mechanically sound, bought a new tire, and had the car insured.

*Paul, Mildred, and Irene O'Leary standing next to Little Firefly*

The three of us took off at once on our trip north, over the Columbia River Highway to Spokane, Washington, then heading northeast to Banff and Lake Louise in Canada. We took time to explore mountain trails and Paul climbed to the summit of Mount St. Piran, an elevation of 8,692 feet, which is 3,000 feet above Lake Louise. Paul slid down a huge snowdrift for nearly 200 feet on the mountainside and said it was great fun. Irene and I went horseback riding over another mountain as well as hiking shorter trails on Mount St. Piran. Then we headed back across British Columbia to Vancouver and enjoyed camping in roadside camps along the way.

It was a long trip of nearly 4,000 miles and Paul repeatedly said he would be happier if we spent more time camping and less traveling. After we left Lake Louise, Paul was ill-tempered and refused to drive the car any more, threatening to take his suitcase and hike to the nearest town and take a train back to San Francisco. His tiff was with Irene and he did not say anything until she asked him to relieve her from driving. Then he flatly refused to have anything to do with the car. We were in the middle of nowhere in a desolate area, which was supposedly infested with rattlesnakes. Irene and I were too scared to sleep in our snake-proof tent. We wanted to drive all night but Irene was so tired of driving that she finally stopped the car. There we sat, miles from God knows where! I could not drive well enough to take a chance of driving on crooked, narrow, rough roads. I had gotten my first driver's license in June, but was very unsure of myself. When Paul refused to drive, we sat there all night.

The next morning, when Irene was driving we passed a rattlesnake. Irene shuddered and steered the car away from it as if she thought it would wreck us if we ran over it. In the afternoon, when Irene became tired, we agreed that I should take a chance of driving the car. I drove it for quite a way and all of our nerves were on edge most of the time for the road was fierce in most places. All at once, the right front wheel struck a pile of loose rock in the middle of the road. Paul yelled, and I yanked the wheel to the left and the car went off the road! There was a deep hole with a wire fence lining it a few feet below the road. Paul leaped out of the car just as it went over. We thought we were goners, but behold, a miracle happened, for that frail-looking fence proved to be very strong. Irene and I climbed out of the car that was pretty well over on its side. Paul walked to a nearby lumber camp and got a team of horses to pull us back onto the road. I was badly shaken and said, "I'll never drive again!" One of the tires was flat and we had it repaired in the next town. After that, Paul drove the car most of the time and even *he* had a broken axle just outside Vancouver. Nevertheless, it was a good trip. At the end of two weeks, Paul returned to San Francisco by train.

Irene and I explored Oregon at every opportunity. Once we went to the coast and tried deep-sea fishing. Irene and I each caught a large salmon for which we had no use, so two fellows on the trip bought them from us. We attended a fiftieth-year celebration in Eugene, Oregon, went to Crater Lake, the lava beds in eastern Oregon, and Mt. Hood. We usually took other nurses with us. We also went to a few public square dances where everyone danced with everyone else, but we made no real acquaintances. Once, two young men invited us to go to the theater in Portland. On the way, they stopped for gas and when the attendant gave back the change, Irene's escort said, "But I gave you a $100 bill and you only gave me change for a ten." They argued and we girls got rather nervous. The fellow insisted that the men go back and look in the cash register, which they finally did. Sure enough, it was $100, and the attendant was most apologetic.

One of my cases at the hospital that fall was a handsome young lawyer. He had had a tonsillectomy but kept hemorrhaging, so I had to watch him carefully. His mother was there with him also, and she liked me. We dated once he was well and he even proposed marriage, but I had no intentions to remain in the West.

# Chapter 8

## An Unexpected Event Changes My Life

*Look not mournfully into the past.*
*It comes not back again.*
*Wisely improve the present. It is thine.*
*Go forth to meet the shadowy future, without fear...*
—Henry Wadsworth Longfellow

On October 29, 1929, the stock market crashed and the Great Depression began. We felt it too, as suddenly people had no money for special nurses. We never ate out when we were not working, just made do with tea and toast, and canned soup cooked on our electric hot plate. I remember the day we took another nurse home to her farm and saw the garden littered with summer squash going to waste. We asked if we could have some and we actually lived on those for weeks.

Back in Greene, the O'Learys sold their farm in November and decided to return West where all their children lived, so Irene urged them to come to Salem. We found a good house for rent, cleaned it up, including the stovepipes and were ready for their furniture when it arrived. We moved in with them.

I was not paid for the last two cases I had, so I decided to go back home. Irene remained, later married, and lived near Salem all her life. I sold my interest in our automobile to Irene and left to visit Paul for a few days. It happened that another nurse decided to go home to Wisconsin at this time, so she and I planned to travel together. Helen Hauge and I left Salem on February 6, 1930, by Greyhound bus. I spent a week with Paul in San Francisco and then I headed for Los

Angeles where I met Helen, who was visiting her sister. We took Grey Line Tours from there to Catalina Island, Pasadena, San Diego, Tijuana, and Aqua Caliente. We wanted to see as much of California as we could, before going back East.

The majority of our journey was by Greyhound bus and our first stop was Phoenix. From there Helen went to a hotel in Globe, Arizona, while I took the longer, more scenic route over the Apache Trail to Globe to meet her. Mine was a most spectacular trip through rugged mountains, but I was carsick much of the way and the bus driver would have to stop and let me out. A passenger offered me brandy from his hip flask and other passengers said it would help me, but I declined every offer of help.

We decided to take the southern route, which included New Mexico, Texas, St. Louis, and Pittsburgh. I was able to buy my tickets from the Yelloway Stage Company at the winter excursion rates, so that helped my pocketbook. When we got to St. Louis, Helen left me to go north to Wisconsin. She wrote later that a young man she had met on our trip kept corresponding with her, and she did eventually marry him.

I reached Binghamton on February 24 after that long, tiring trip and my parents met me at the bus station. They were aghast at my loss of weight at the end of those eighteen days and nights of travel, but I was soon back in shape. I felt that I was fortunate to be able to travel and see as much as I did in the twenty months since I left home.

I returned to private duty nursing and had cases in Greene and Norwich steadily. I was taking care of a boy in the old Norwich hospital at the time of the move into the newly built hospital. A case I found hard to forget was taking care of a pneumonia patient who lived on a farm near Mt. Upton. My father drove me over there. The patient was an eighty-year-old woman. Her daughter, who was a middle-aged spinster, lived with her and the mother's second husband. He was as young as the daughter was. The mother told me she did the housework and her daughter helped her stepfather do all the farm work. I was on duty twenty-four hours a day for eleven days and did not go to bed the entire time I was there. I sat on a straight hard chair just outside the door to my patient's room at night. I slept with my head on my arms on a small stand with a smelly kerosene lamp on it. From the first, I took over washing the dishes and little by little got the house cleaned up. When I left, my patient was sitting in a large chair, her hair freshly shampooed and she looked very peaceful. However, three days later, she was found dead in bed of heart failure, so I was told.

My brother Paul wrote that he had lost his job and for several months had looked and looked for a permanent job elsewhere in California. Everyone was experiencing hard times and finding short-term employment here and there was discouraging, but it kept hope alive for a while. After being away from Greene for nearly three and one-half years, he decided to return home. Paul's trusted Harley Davidson motorcycle was his mode of transportation. He pawned everything that he could not take with him. On October 26, 1930, he left Greenville, California, where he had had temporary employment. It was a hard, tedious journey across the Rocky Mountains and there was not one day that he did not suffer extremely from the cold. He must have been quite a remarkable sight as he wore all the clothes he could pile onto himself. When he reached Greene, after a long and dangerous sixteen-day trip across the country, Paul was practically broke. What a grand reunion we all had! How thankful we were that he arrived safely. He rode that trusty motorcycle 3,400 miles, and 1,800 miles were unpaved roads. "Yellowbird" averaged forty-eight miles per gallon and his entire trip cost exactly $50. However, he suffered terribly. When he crossed the salt flats near the Great Salt Lake, he had to stop occasionally to run around and jump up and down at a great rate in order to get warm. He had some narrow escapes but only one spill due to the loose gravel and sandy road surfaces. Paul kept a detailed diary of his exploits and for days, he shared one story after another.

Thanksgiving was the first one in five years that we were all together. Mama and Papa were so thankful that Paul and I were home safely from our adventures in the West. But, due to the Depression, the future held little promise of finding work. According to the newspapers the unemployment situation was getting worse everywhere. Work was slack for me and I had not had any work for nearly a month. Paul tried to get a job in all the nearby communities, but it was useless. In desperation, he decided to depend upon trapping animals during the winter to earn what little he could from selling the fur. He helped Papa with the farm chores, but continued to be downhearted about not finding work.

Nursing assignments were not as frequent as I would like, so it was not long before I began to be restless. I knew it was time to get back into institutional nursing. Therefore, I applied to the U.S. Navy Nurse Corps. My previous experience, my age *and* being single resulted in my being accepted. I started work in mid-February of 1931. I was assigned to the U.S. Naval Hospital in Brooklyn, New York and was immediately put in charge of the surgical ward, which held 120 beds, the largest of its kind in the United States. Spinal anesthesia was the only anesthesia given. I had several corpsmen assistants.

At the end of May, I was transferred to night duty on a medical ward, working from 11 p.m. to 7 a.m. An adjoining ward had all ambulatory patients so only one corpsman was stationed there. He had to report to me and I would look in on the ward occasionally. He came over to my ward first, to see the new nurse. After that, he kept finding excuses to drop by, first to borrow something, then to bring me a milkshake, a book to read, or to talk. I was more annoyed than pleased.

A young friend of my family, who had graduated from NYU, was working in the banking district and he invited me to spend Memorial Day boating on Long Island Sound. We took a picnic lunch and spent the day in our swimsuits in the bright warm sun and we got terrific sunburns. I went on duty that night looking like a beet. Well, that corpsman from next door was most solicitous and would have been my slave if I had let him. I finally had to tell him to go over where he belonged. However, every night was the same.

One morning, as four or five of us nurses were walking down the long hall to go off duty, that corpsman intercepted us. With eyes only for me, he said, "Here Miss English. These are for you," and he thrust a bouquet of American Beauty roses into my hands, turned, and fled. Well, I was embarrassed and the girls were curious. I said, "His name is Jimmy Cochrane, and he is *not my* corpsman!" Those roses lasted an unbelievably long time in a vase beside my bed. They were the first thing I saw when I wakened and the last thing I saw when I retired. They seemed to be trying to say something to me, but I would not listen.

One day after I came off night duty, I was walking across the Brooklyn Bridge with another nurse when there coming toward us was that Jimmy Cochrane and a buddy. They stopped to talk to us and finally walked along the same way with us. That was the beginning for Jimmy and me. We began to explore all the historical places of interest together, museums, and parks where he read poetry to me while I manicured his fingernails. We rode endless miles on the subways just talking. Every suppertime he would call me while I was eating in the nurses' dining room, and I would go to the phone booth to talk more. All the months that we went together, we never ran into anyone from the hospital. I never mentioned him to any of the nurses, nor did he tell any of his buddies about seeing me. We never left the hospital at the same time or returned on the same bus. We met on the Brooklyn Bridge and came back over the Manhattan Bridge and one pair of shoes after another wore out.

\* \* \*

When the weather grew cold, we decided to get married. I bought our matching wedding rings and had announcements printed. We took the train to Binghamton on the first Saturday in November, where Jimmy met my parents for the first time. Sunday was spent getting acquainted and showing him around Greene. We were married on Monday, the ninth of November in 1931 in the Immaculate Conception Church.

*Jimmy and Mildred Cochrane's wedding photo.*
*Tyl Bollman and Paul English attendants.*

My brother, Paul, and my longtime friend Tyl Bollman stood up with us. The wedding was simple enough and was far from being a big affair, because I did not want a big fuss of any kind. We were married at the foot of the altar because Jimmy was not a Catholic. The church was about half-full with neighbors, friends, and relatives. After the ceremony was over, we four went to the local photographer (Charles R. Wheeler) to have our wedding portrait taken.

Jimmy and I returned to Brooklyn on the midnight train from Binghamton and he went directly back on duty at 7 a.m. I went to the nearby Grand Hotel to sleep for the day, before returning to the hospital. There I gave each of my special friends an announcement. They were thunderstruck. Within a day or so, I turned in my resignation for December 1. I wish I could have kept my job, but nurses of that era were no longer employable once they were married.

During the next three weeks, Jimmy and I hunted for an apartment on our time off. It was very discouraging as they were all so cheerless, too much like living in a kitchen, or too expensive. At last, we found a one-room furnished apartment in Brooklyn for $40 per month, and there we spent our first night together, three weeks after our marriage! Then I tried to find work under my married name, but no hospitals were hiring married nurses. The Depression was getting worse. Dr. and Mary Ann McCoy, newly married like we were, lived on the floor above us and she and I spent our days looking for food bargains. They found a cheaper place to live, and then we did.

Time went by quickly. Jimmy's friends were in and out and so were mine. Our little haven was like a home away from home to them. On warm weekends, Jimmy and I hiked up the aqueduct, or along river trails, with our knapsacks on our backs. We were very much in love and content with just being together.

On April 4, 1933, we bought a 1927 Dodge sedan for $45. Jimmy's service was up on April 15. Three days later, we loaded all our possessions into it and headed for Greene, where we stayed with my parents for the next thirteen months. Jimmy had taken a course in poultry raising at New York University and decided to go into the poultry farming business. Every day we looked for a place to settle but we had no luck. Papa came to our rescue and deeded seven acres of land on the Coventry Road to us. Jimmy immediately bought lumber, built, and equipped five brooder houses for 1,500 baby chicks (which arrived in May). We also planted a vegetable garden.

From May until November, I supervised in the hospital in Norwich (under my maiden name), until the supervisor learned that I was married, so I had to quit. Fortunately, I could still do private duty nursing, which I did for the next six months. Every paycheck went to buy food for those chickens. I rode to Norwich on the 5 a.m. train and returned on the evening bus. One bitter subzero day that winter, my train had difficulty getting up steam and it took more than two hours to go those twenty-two miles to Norwich. There was no taxi and during the mile walk to the hospital, my legs got so badly chilled that the veins were red-streaked and painful for months. How I wished I could wear trousers as I had done out West, but trousers were not acceptable women's wear in those days.

In September, we rented St. Johns' henhouse below the village and moved the pullets there. When the chickens started laying eggs, I helped candle the eggs, packing them into crates according to size to be shipped by truck to New York City.

We started building a Cape Cod house that September (1933) and moved into it nine months later. Our one and one-half story house included a kitchen with built-in eating area, a living room with brick fireplace, dining room, and small office on the first floor. A beautiful wide staircase led to the second floor, which consisted of one bathroom, three bedrooms, and lots of closet space. The furnace in the basement burned coal, so Jimmy built a coal bin. I helped build the foundation, nailed on drywall, sanded and painted the woodwork at every opportunity. We did much of the work inside after we moved in. For many months, we climbed a ladder to get to the bathroom on the second floor. I felt I was in seventh heaven when the stairs were eventually built. Twice I slipped through the subfloor upstairs and through the plasterboard ceiling of the room underneath. We had very little money for furniture but found just what we needed at local auctions.

*The house we built on Coventry Road*

We moved into our home at 20 Coventry Road on May 28, 1934. It was the first house inside the incorporated village of Greene on the south side of the road and directly across from the Sylvan Lawn Cemetery. The only farms between us and where I had grown up on the Van Valkenburgh farm were the Pratt farm on the left side of the Coventry Road and the Curtis farm on the right. Many years later, our house became the rectory for the Catholic Church.

Once the construction was well underway on our house, Jimmy started building a large henhouse to accommodate the chickens when they were old enough to move out of the five brooder houses. We had a dance in it before the hens were old enough to occupy it. The first dance was so successful that we had a second dance there as well. Friends gave us a surprise housewarming party and we received many useful gifts.

\* \* \*

In the early morning of July 8, 1935, Greene had the greatest flood in her history. We were completely unaware of it until a frantic phone call came from friends. Frances Hunsicker's house at 46 North Chenango Street was flooded and she asked if they could come to our house. We drove down to met them at the foot of Washington Street and waited anxiously for them to cross the river in a rowboat. Both approaches to the bridge were under water and no traffic was allowed on the bridge until late in the day. The flood caused untold property damage and a number of lives were lost. A series of cloudbursts in the northern part of the state flooded streams and lakes causing several dams to burst. The floodwaters gushed down the Chenango Valley leaving devastation in its wake. Within twelve hours, the waters started to recede and then the cleanup began. We were thankful to have built on high ground.

\* \* \*

Then our children came along. I gave birth to a ten-pound boy on March 31, 1936. We named our son Thomas English Cochrane. Both children were born in Norwich Hospital. I had a postpartum hemorrhage in the delivery room following Tommy's birth, the worse ever seen there. Everyone was panicky and rushing around and the chief surgeon was called in. I kept asking if I were going to die, but no one paid any attention to me. Then in my subconscious, I heard (or sensed) the words "Be still" and immediately I calmed down and said in my mind, "Into Thy Hands I commend myself" and I passed out.

Nineteen months later our second child was born on October 25, 1937, one month premature. Dr. Chapin rushed me to Norwich early that morning just as the sun was rising. He stopped to pick up my dear friend Frances Hunsicker who tended to my needs in the backseat of his car. Dr. Chapin drove as fast as he dared for he feared for my life as he recognized my dangerous condition immediately. I, too, recognized placenta praevia as a complication of pregnancy that was often fatal. Frances did her best to keep me calm, and I prayed desperately for my life and that of my unborn child. Jorette was a caesarian birth and we had special nurses afterward for one week. I had to stay in the hospital for two weeks. The hospital bill came to $90.55, the special nurses $54, and additional bills from two surgeons, Dr. Chapin and another hospital doctor. It was two years before we were able to pay off all the expenses for her birth. Dr.

Chapin said, "Young woman! That is all the babies you should have. Another pregnancy might be the death of you or of me."

\* \* \*

Shortly before Jorette was born, my brother Paul announced that he was engaged to Genevieve McCombs. I remembered her from Teacher's Training Class, but did not know Paul was seeing her. He said they had dated for a month or so and that he proposed to Genevieve at the Labor Day Picnic. Not only that, they planned to get married on Saturday, October 9, 1937. Father Lyons officiated and the ceremony took place in the Oxford Rectory. Jimmy and Genevieve's sister, Gertrude Coleman, stood up with them. After the wedding ceremony, they came back to Papa and Mama's home for a small reception for the immediate families before going on a four-day honeymoon.

\* \* \*

The following years were busy, happy ones, working together and watching our children grow. Cochrane's Poultry Farm was a breeding farm for white leghorn chickens. The incubator room where hundreds of baby chicks were hatched each year was over the garage. Brooder houses for the young chicks were in line south of the building, and the large henhouse was located on the west side of the property line. Once the buildings were constructed, our poultry farm kept Jimmy busy breeding, raising, and selling young chicks as well as eggs.

In the summer of 1939, we took our first vacation on a trip through Maine, New Hampshire, and Vermont. We left Jorette with my parents and took Tommy with us. It was a new adventure for us, traveling in our pickup truck with a three-year-old. We had a mattress in the back and at night, a tarpaulin draped over four stakes in the corners making it a comfortable "tent." Everyone we camped near thought it a clever idea.

When we were about to leave the campground in Bar Harbor, I took Tommy to the rest room, then got into the car and let him play on the bumper next to his dad, who was chatting with a neighbor. Jimmy got into the car and said, "Where's Tom?" I said, "He was there with you playing on the bumper." Now, Tommy was nowhere to be seen. Jimmy called and called and all the campers searched their tents. I went back to the rest room that was quite a distance away, but he was not there either. By then everyone was panicky and had the same thought, as our site was the one closest to the highway. Perhaps someone passing could have snatched up that cute little boy. Ever since the disappearance of the son of Charles Lindbergh, kidnapping was on people's minds. Oh, did I ever pray! Someone suggested calling the state police. I went back to the rest room once more and yelled loudly into the woods at the rear and to my relief, Tommy came running, "Here I am, Mama!"

*  *  *

Ten years had passed since the stock market crashed and the economy had not improved as much as we had hoped it would. Egg prices were only 15 to 25 cents per dozen. The white leghorn pullets were selling for only $1.00 apiece. Paul was of the opinion that too many people were in the poultry business, which was keeping the profit down.

From April 1, 1940, to April 7, 1942, Jimmy was a member of the Board of Trustees of the Village of Greene. He was popular and made friends quickly. One year he served on the committee in charge of the Labor Day Community Picnic. He was active in the Masons and people in the community thought highly of him.

# Chapter 9

# The War Years

*Be still, sad heart! and cease repining;*
*Behind the clouds is the sun still shining;*
*Thy fate is the common fate of all,*
*Into each life some rain must fall,*
*Some days must be dark and dreary.*
—Henry Wadsworth Longfellow

In 1941, war clouds in Europe brought out patriotism in American men. Jimmy and Raymond Beckwith went up to northern New York State for a short time to work on building Camp Drum, a military training camp. They came home weekends. Then, Jimmy and Jack Bigelow heard of defense jobs in Virginia and Maryland. There was an urgent need for men to help enlarge the facilities at the Aberdeen Proving Grounds in Maryland. The pay was $1.00 an hour, so five men from Greene went down to work on a similar project near the Aberdeen Proving Grounds. One spring weekend, we five wives drove down to see them. There was so much work to do and the pay better than in the poultry business, so the Alfred Turners and Jimmy and I decided to move down there.

We sold our hens, rented the house, stored our furniture and left for Charlestown, Maryland. The men found a cottage where four children and we four adults lived from July to November 1941. We went swimming every day that summer in the Charlestown River. When a second cottage was available, Al and Lillian and their sons Gerry and Phil moved into it.

Our cottage was too cold for winter so we rented a house in a new housing development in Havre de Grace, across the river from Charlestown. We had our furniture moved down from Greene. In the evening, we would sit and listen to the radio and I began to crochet rag rugs to help pass the time.

Then, on December 7, we were out for a Sunday afternoon ride, when a news announcer interrupted the radio program with the startling news of the bombing of Pearl Harbor. Tom and Jorette were in the backseat of the car. I can remember them saying, "What's the matter?" Jimmy and I could not believe what we were hearing. Who could imagine at that moment, an event so far away would change our lives forever? It was a day that none of us would ever forget.

In Havre de Grace, Dr. Jastram learned that I was an RN so he came and asked if I would consider taking charge of a new First Aid Station on the Campgrounds. As a civilian nurse, I would be working for the three insurance companies that took care of the civilian workers. I began work in April and worked there for three months.

It was next to impossible to find a reliable person to take care of our children. Finally, someone sent a high school girl to me. Well! Every day when I got home from work, the children were dirty from head to toe. One day, a neighbor found Tommy and her son were under our house playing with matches. Another day, the girl baked a pie and set it hot out of the oven onto the seat of my prized antique kitchen chair and burned the seat. The next time, she had mopped the kitchen floor and I never saw a floor look worse. A few days later, I opened the door when I returned from work and found water from the toilet bowl had overflowed and the house was flooded. She had put large pieces of orange rind in the toilet, which repeated flushing could not dislodge. I exclaimed, "That's the last straw!" I could not stand those frustrations one more hour, so I told her to pack her things and leave at once. I was actually livid and had to brace myself against the wall to keep from falling. That evening, Jimmy phoned my parents and asked if they could keep the children. Of course, they were delighted, so we packed up their belongings and left for Greene early the next morning. That was Memorial Day and we encountered parades in each village we drove through. We spent very little time in Greene as we returned to Havre de Grace the same night in order to get to work by morning. Mama enrolled Tommy in the Greene School the next day.

I could now concentrate on my work and not worry about the children. Many minor accidents occurred among the 1,000 construction workers at the camp in spite of strict safety rules. I had to keep records on everything from an infected splinter to skinned shins. For lacerations requiring stitches, I would phone one of the two town doctors who came on call. I remember a man who *was scalped* when a board struck him edgewise from above. The scalp hung by only an inch strip to his skull but the doctor came at once and attached it successfully.

The First Aid Station was so near the Army base that I could see the raw "just out of high school" recruits come, train, and leave as rugged men. I would see them dressed in full gear marching off on week-long treks in all kinds of weather to "play war," then return limping on blistered feet, bedraggled and weather-beaten. As I was the only female around they often came to me for aspirin, or to remove slivers and for simple remedies, which would otherwise take hours to get waiting in the sickbay lineup. I liked helping the young recruits, so would gladly attend to their minor needs although we all knew that we were off-limits to each other.

When this part of the camp was finished, my First Aid Station was torn down and I was transferred to a second one in a distant part of the grounds. This was more spacious as it was in the house that had once been the homestead on the farm. It was evident that this had been a beautiful farm, and no doubt the owner was paid plenty to sell it. Corn in the cornfields was knee high when leveled by bulldozers for rows of new Army barracks. Each day Dr. Jastram would rescue luscious strawberries from the large bed near our First Aid Station. This second job also lasted three months.

Jimmy voluntarily enlisted in the Seabees after recruiters told of the need for a militarized Naval Construction Battalion to build advance bases in the war zones. The Navy urged men experienced in construction to adapt their civilian skills to military needs. The first Seabees were technically a support group, responsible for building harbors, airfields, and bases. Many of the recruits were older experienced men. In October 1942, Jimmy and I returned to Greene to attend to personal business and await his orders.

We were so happy to be moving back into our own home after renting it for eighteen months while working in Maryland. However, we had to stay with my parents for three months until our tenants moved out in January 1943. Then our happiness was short lived, as it was not long before Jimmy's orders to leave for training in Alaska arrived.

After Jimmy left, I started at once to relieve the three shifts at the Greene Hospital and continued to do so until the end of 1944. Due to the war, married women were no longer frowned upon for working outside the home and nurses were in demand even in our small community. The Hill Brothers had recently bought Bessie Turner's small private hospital, renovated it, and began operating the Greene Hospital on January 1, 1943. There were no RNs available to cover the shifts. What could be more convenient than to find work at a hospital a mile from home? And with Mama and Papa close by, I had no worries about childcare.

About this same time, Papa started talking about retiring from farming. In January of 1943, he surprised us by purchasing a house on the corner of Chenango and Foundry Streets across from the Mobil Gas station. He paid $2,650 for the house and needed to build a small garage for his car. Papa and Mama did not move in until 1944 as there were tenants living there.

In March 1944, Jimmy came home on a 30-day furlough from his training in Kodiak, Alaska. It was a wonderful month, perhaps the best of all we had together and the time went way too fast. Due to the uncertainty of the war, we decided to sell the brooder houses and poultry equipment to Courtney Bryant, who also rented the henhouse for four months. Like so many other families, we had to put our dreams on hold until the war would end.

*Mildred with Tommy and Jorette - 1944*

Not long after Jimmy left for California, my parents sold their farm to Harry Wortsman. They had lived there for 23 years and been very happy on that farm. They stored their furniture in my garage and moved in with me in June until the house in the village was ready to occupy. I started helping the County Nurse with her home nursing cases and Mama took care of the children when I was working. Papa was busy renovating the house on 16 South Chenango Street. In my free time, I helped him paint and helped Mama select wallpaper for her new home.

In May, I sold our car to Sam Shabus for $400. I had no use for it as I had no confidence in my driving ability and it looked like the war was going to be a long one. I needed the money to pay off feed bills from the poultry business, so every cent went to pay our debts.

Sometime after my parents moved into their new home, my back started to give out. It got worse after I fell down the full length of the stairs early one morning when hurrying to answer the phone. I wrenched my back so badly that for the next six weeks, the children did all the house chores. Tommy (age 7) helped do the laundry and Jorette

(5½) took the grocery list to town and my parents brought the groceries home. Jorette would heat her little toy flatiron and place it on my back as I spent most of the time in pain on the couch. Dr. Chapin gave me B-12 shots, but they did no good. The chiropractor helped some. After six weeks of bed rest, I was able to work for the first time.

There came a day in September 1944 that completely devastated me. I was canning tomato juice when the mail came. In the mailbox was a letter from Jimmy. I sat down to read it. Well, my life suddenly fell apart. Jimmy wrote that he had met someone else, had been unfaithful, and he ended by asking for a divorce. I don't know how I ever finished canning that juice. That evening the children and I prayed harder than we ever had before. When I phoned him in California and said I would come out (knowing the train ride would kill me due to the extreme pain in my back), he said no—it would make no difference.

More letters followed with no change. Then the Navy shipped him to Guam in the Pacific and we seldom heard from him. I was beside myself. I thought I would die–and I could not tell a soul. Only the children kept me going from day to day. Although very young, they were my crutches. I knew I had to do something, but I did not know what to do.

A few days later, I was sitting outside on the stone wall with the sun on my back trying to reach down, without bending, to pull up a few tall weeds among my flowers. The pain was so intense, I cried and I had difficulty in climbing the three steps into the kitchen, and then making my way to the living room to lie down. My parents took things into their own hands when I called them. They took me to see an osteopath in Binghamton. They had to help me out of the car and into Dr. Thompson's office. He gave me just one adjustment to my back and neck, and I screamed. However, I stood up straight and walked out as if I had never had anything wrong with me. I was able to return to work at the hospital and praised God for healing.

Soon after that, the children and I were listening to the radio one evening, when I heard an appeal for civilian registered nurses who were desperately needed at the Rhoads Army Hospital near Utica, because of a lack of Army nurses. That appeal seemed to be made directly to me. I listened carefully for the next few nights and made a decision. This was a direct answer to my prayers. I needed to help others who were more in need than I was, so I wrote them. In a short time, I received an answer saying I could start in January. I sold our brooder stoves and paid off some more bills from the poultry business, and knowing I could cut expenses, I set about closing up my house for the winter. Then the three of us went down to stay with my parents. During the month of November, I relieved the school nurse who was on maternity leave, and worked regularly at the Greene Hospital from 4 p.m. to midnight. My total income in 1944 was $2,381.23.

I was eager to begin working in a military hospital, but in doing so my children and I had to be separated again. I arranged to place Jorette in St. John's Home and School in Utica, which cared for orphaned girls of all ages. However, due to the war they accepted a few children whose parent was in a similar situation to mine. Tommy stayed with my parents. Jorette and I took the bus to Utica, and I remember how terrified she was when I left her with a nun after signing her in and taking her to the dormitory that she would share with nineteen other girls. I assured her that I would be back in a few days and that I would call her every night. As I left, I prayed that my decision to work in the army hospital was the best one for all of us.

When I arrived at Rhoads Army Hospital, I was finger-printed and processed late that afternoon and immediately put on duty at 8 p.m. My next shift after a couple of hours sleep was from 7 a.m. to 3:30 p.m. WOW! Planeloads of prisoners of war arrived daily. The soldiers were evaluated and then sent to specialty hospitals elsewhere in the United States. Rhoads kept all skin disease cases. Those were the patients with whom I worked. The soldiers came looking like skeletons, nervous and shaky, hair falling out and full of sores. Men from the Pacific area who had lived in wet boots for weeks at a time had bad cases of "jungle rot." What a joy it was to see those boys gain weight and improve mentally and physically each day from good food, vitamins, medications, and bed rest. Their hair grew in; sparkle came back into their eyes and skin improved from the soaks and other treatments. Once again they became young and vibrant—truly a miracle.

I phoned Jorette daily at first and went to see her on my day off. We went to Greene on the 6 p.m. bus three times while we were in Utica and once to Little Falls to see my friend Tyl and her family. In May, the nuns chose Jorette to crown the statue of the Blessed Virgin on the feast of the Immaculate Conception. It was a perfect May day for the lovely ceremony and Jorette looked so sweet in her white dress. She received her first communion a week later.

Shortly after the war ended, we civilian nurses were discharged. July 4 was my last day at Rhoads after five months of duty there. The next day, I picked up Jorette and we headed home on the bus to Greene. Within a few days, I went back to work at the Greene Hospital relieving the three shifts each week.

Now that the war was over, I found myself unprepared to resume my life and announce to people that I was no longer married. I wanted to put the war behind me but my life was permanently changed. I would no longer have a traditional family life. All the demands of motherhood remained as well as that of supporting the family. I was glad I had chosen nursing as my profession and knew that I could get a job anywhere. But how would my children fit in? My mind was in turmoil....What was the Lord's Will for my life?

It was not until the war ended in the Pacific that I finally told my parents the real reason I was so despondent. Three months later, they persuaded me to spend the winter in Florida with them. My parents thought a change of scenery might help me come to terms with my broken heart. They rented an apartment in Kissimmee, Florida, and I started the children in school there a week after we arrived. Somehow, the owner of the Kissimmee General Hospital learned there was a new RN in town, contacted me, and offered me a job working the day shift. When I said I did not want to work in Florida as I was there on vacation, the owner replied, "Oh, please come and help us. We are desperate!"

The hospital was full of patients and understaffed. I worked mostly twelve hours *every* day from November 19 to the middle of March when we left for home. About all I saw of Florida that winter was on our way into and out of the state and the scenery on my mile walk to and from the hospital each day.

Most of the patients were elderly. Attached to the rear of the hospital by a wooden ramp was a barn-like annex for the blacks. When I discovered that, I was appalled by the lack of care they received. Therefore, that was where I spent the last hours of each day on my own time, and the patients really appreciated the attention I gave them. One very ill man was an elderly minister and every sentence he uttered contained words of wisdom. I wish I could recall what we talked about, but I remember how blessed I felt after leaving his bedside. One patient was on a cot on a shabby side porch with the rain almost reaching him. The winter winds swirled around this shack and I wondered how any of the patients survived.

In December, I received divorce papers from a lawyer in Reno, Nevada. Jimmy was out of the service and had gone there to get a quick divorce, so I had no choice but to let him go. Thus I signed those necessary papers and life ended for me that day before Christmas 1945.

\* \* \*

As spring approached, the hospital owner asked me to stay on and be in full charge. She would pay me *anything* to stay. At the same time, letters were flying back and forth between the Greene Hospital and me urging me to come home and take charge as superintendent there. Maud Mosher was nearing the end of her days and could not hang on much longer. I said NO to both positions as I did not want to be that tied down, not when I had two children to raise.

Before going home to Greene, I had one bridge to cross. Papa and Mama and I decided it would be best to send a notice regarding my divorce to the newspaper in Greene so the shock would be over before I reached home in March. I never talked about it and not one soul in all my acquaintance ever dared mention it to me, although I suspected they wanted to and I felt their sympathy. To shield myself from the pain, I receded into a shell of my own making and cut off contact with my close friends. My children and work and my faith kept me going. I believe that of all life's blessings, work is one of the greatest. In time, the burden of grief and loneliness was lifted from my heart.

When I came to terms with my heartbreak, I decided my future and my children's would be going home to Greene. My roots were there. With the help of my parents and my brother Paul, I hoped Tommy and Jorette would develop the same values that I learned growing up in Greene. I had traveled across the United States and worked in many places but not one had tempted me to put down roots and stay. My children were 6th generation residents going back to Nathanial English. Greene was our home. When we left Florida that spring, I was at peace in my heart knowing my decision was for the best. I would no longer look back at what was now lost to me, but would look ahead to raising my family in the security of my hometown.

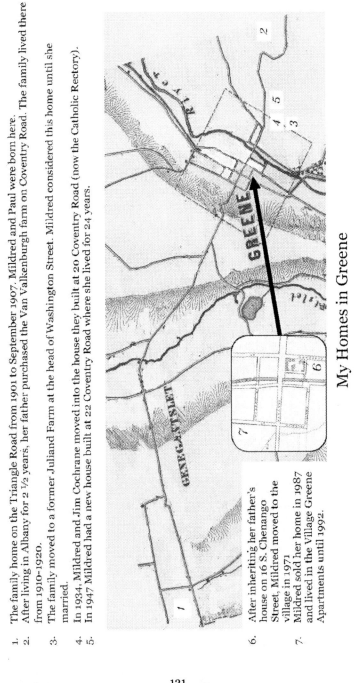

## My Homes in Greene

1. The family home on the Triangle Road from 1901 to September 1907. Mildred and Paul were born here.
2. After living in Albany for 2 ½ years, her father purchased the Van Valkenburgh farm on Coventry Road. The family lived there from 1910-1920.
3. The family moved to a former Juliand Farm at the head of Washington Street. Mildred considered this home until she married.
4. In 1934, Mildred and Jim Cochrane moved into the house they built at 20 Coventry Road (now the Catholic Rectory).
5. In 1947 Mildred had a new house built at 22 Coventry Road where she lived for 24 years.

6. After inheriting her father's house on 16 S. Chenango Street, Mildred moved to the village in 1971
7. Mildred sold her home in 1987 and lived in the Village Greene Apartments until 1992.

# Chapter 10

## Returning Home to Greene

*Four things a man must learn to do*
*If he would make his record true:*
*To think without confusion clearly;*
*To love his fellow-men sincerely;*
*To act from honest motives purely;*
*To trust in God and Heaven securely.*
—Henry Van Dyke

We arrived home on March 18, 1946, and were once again back in our own house. Two days later, the Hill brothers, who owned the Greene Hospital, came and *begged* me to take charge of Greene's nineteen-bed hospital. They were desperate, so I finally agreed, "but only until someone else could be found." I started to work on March 22.

The two-story house, garage, large henhouse, and three acres of land were really more than a family of three needed, so Papa suggested building a smaller, one-story house on a half-acre lot next door to the house I owned. He drew up the plans and staked it out. In June, Papa had the cellar dug and started building the house. I sold the two-story house in 1947 for $10,000.

Our new home at 22 Coventry Road was ready to move into at the end of May 1947. It had three bedrooms, one bathroom, a kitchen, living room, dining room and a full basement. It was perfect for the three of us. Papa built the garage a year later and Tom (age 11) painted it. I needed a garage for the children's bicycles, a power lawn mower, garden cart, and tools. Everyone encouraged me to buy a car, but we got along without one until Tom was old enough to get a driver's license.

*My second home on Coventry Road*

Jorette and Tommy were nine and one-half and eleven when we moved into our new home. Our family was somewhat of a rarity having a working mom and no father at home. I had to teach them to take care of themselves because I was frequently at work when the children left for school in the morning or when they arrived home in the afternoon. We kept the house key under the doormat so they could enter the house if they arrived home before I did. Many times, they had to get themselves ready for school when I worked the day shift. The children rode the school bus to and from school, whereas I would walk the mile to work and back, which I did not mind doing considering I had walked to school and to work all of my life.

Throughout grammar school, my children stayed with Mama and Papa during holidays and summer vacation. During the school year, they walked to my parent's home at noon recess as Mama always cooked the main meal of the day at noon. At suppertime, the children and I lived on soup and sandwiches. I tried not to work the 3 to 11 shift so I could be home in the evening with my children. When unexpected hospital duties prevented me from being home for supper, Tom and Jorette had to fend for themselves. By the time they were in junior high school, they were better cooks than I was—and capable of doing anything. I taught them to keep the house as orderly as I would. I had several rules: their beds must be made before leaving the house, their clothes hung up, and no dirty dishes left in the sink. They took responsibility well, and oh, how I appreciated it! Consequently, Tom and Jorette grew up to be quite independent.

After we settled into our new home, I immediately began to design the layout for our yard and garden. I designed flowerbeds so that the flowers bloomed from April until late October, filling our yard with profusion of brilliant color. The children and I did all of the digging, planting shrubs and bushes, and landscaping ourselves.

I loved gardening and was never happier than tending to my flowers. I never neglected my flowerbeds no matter how tired I was when I got home from work. I learned to take a catnap for 20 minutes and then I would find an hour or so of solitude pulling weeds, thinning perennials, or snipping off dead and dying blooms. Any feelings I had of loneliness were, for the most part, taken care of by my flowers from the first crocus to the last chrysanthemums and in books the rest of the year. I believe the closest to true peace in my life was when I worked in my flowerbeds.

Early each spring, I looked forward to the flower and bulb catalogs that arrived in the mail. I read Burpee Seed Catalogs from cover to cover, deciding what new perennials to order. One year I planted a trumpet vine by the back door, gently tying the green shoots to the trellis. Over the years, that vine grew up to the roof and was breathtaking when it was in bloom.

One year, Tommy tried growing a few peanuts and although I doubted they would grow in our northern climate, he did have some success. Another time, he went in for watermelons and had so many that he sold quite a few to the local grocery stores. We tried kohlrabi, Chinese cabbage, and little tomatoes. For several years, Tommy and Jorette raised strawberries and sold them for fifty cents a quart to earn money. We had a raspberry patch, a grape arbor, apple and plum trees and a large garden. We grew every vegetable we liked and always had more than Papa and Mama and my family needed. What we did not eat, can or freeze, the children sold at a roadside stand. As for all the work, I never minded the work involved in planting and maintaining a garden. After supper, I would do the hand weeding while Tom did the cultivating with the wheel cultivator.

Since I had always enjoyed traveling, I wanted my children to develop a sense of adventure and see other places. Therefore, Mama and the three of us took a three-day trip to New York City by night bus from Binghamton, arriving there at six in the morning. After tramping about in the rain all day sightseeing we were exhausted so did not get up early the next morning. Tommy (12) shared Mama's hotel room and Jorette (10) was with me in the adjoining room. When I awoke, Jorette was neither with me nor in the other room. After looking all over for her, I was frantic when she could not be found. The maid and elevator man searched with us! "Oh," said the maid, "Never let a child out of your sight. She could be snatched by someone and you'd never see her again." I went down to the lobby a second time to look out on the street—and there she was sitting in a big chair facing the door just watching people come and go. The next day, she scared us again. As we exited a subway train, the door quickly closed leaving Jorette alone inside. The train pulled away as my heart almost stopped beating. Fortunately, another passenger saw what happened and told Jorette to get off at the next stop. There she waited for us to appear on the next train. Looking back, I can see how the Lord was with me—and with us—in both situations.

* * *

Our family life revolved around my job at the hospital, school, my parents, and Paul. My brother, the children and I attended the Catholic Church every Sunday as well as on Holy Days like Ascension Thursday and All Saints Day. Paul usually picked up the three of us on Sunday morning and drove us to church. We always sat in the same pew with my mother who arrived at church earlier than we did. Then, after Mass, all of us would go to Mama and Papa's house and the children and I would often stay for dinner. We would all read Papa's newspaper that he had read while we were at Mass and then discuss what was happening in the world.

Our religion was not just a Sunday ritual. We followed the doctrines of the church but I also encouraged the children to respect the beliefs of others. I taught the children to say grace before eating and to recite their prayers before going to bed at night. As small children, their bedtime prayer was *"Now I lay me down to sleep, I pray the Lord my soul to keep. If I should die before I wake, I pray the Lord my soul to take. If I should live for other days, I pray the Lord to guide my ways."* Once they received their First Communion, I instructed them to recite the Lord's Prayer, Hail Mary, and the Apostles Creed and pray for the blessing of God upon others. We occasionally prayed the rosary together.

I believed it was my duty as a Christian mother to raise my children with the knowledge of God's loving and forgiving nature, to honor Him, and to serve Him. I wanted them to know that God loves them and gives each person unique abilities to live as God created them to live.

When Tommy was about ten years old, he became an altar boy. The Mass was in Latin in those days and Tommy learned the traditional Latin responses quite easily. Both children were confirmed into the Catholic Church when they became teenagers. Greene was not a Catholic community, so there were only about eight or ten other Catholic children in their grades.

I grew up believing that religion is necessary in our lives. It gives us something—a spiritual quality we can get in no other way—it elevates us. The various denominations make little difference for each serves its own purpose and reaches those souls that no one would. I doubt if the rituals of each church can surely matter in the great scheme of things.

I never saw a reason for religious discrimination. My father was a Baptist, my mother a Catholic, and most of our friends were of the Protestant faith. My brother and I were brought up in Mama's faith and my children naturally followed me. There was never any trouble in my family over religious differences and why should there be? I always considered myself most fortunate and honored to belong to so old a church. There were times one winter when my troubles seemed about to swamp me. When I would step inside a Catholic Church, sit, and think for a long time, I somehow would find relief even when I could not pray. I have heard sermons in Protestant churches that far excelled any heard in mine and gave me food for thought for a long time. Later in life, I pursued a closer walk with the Lord and I started reading the Bible in search of the truth.

\* \* \*

In the years when the children were going through the comic book stage and thought that the only interesting books were the Hardy Boys or Nancy Drew mystery stories, I felt the urge to do something about it. They were missing so much by not reading the classics and I felt they would not be able to catch up later in their lives. It was not enough to place books before their eyes or take them to the library, so I began reading aloud to them while Tommy worked on his hobbies of making clay models of medieval forts, or building wooden models of historic wooden ships. Jorette made doll clothes, worked on weaving squares for an afghan, or worked on her post card collection. I introduced them to *Treasure Island, Tom Sawyer,* and *Huckleberry Finn* and then branched out to more challenging literature such as *Twenty Thousand Leagues under the Sea* and *Tales of King Arthur.* As they got older, we had a lot of fun vagabonding round the world with Richard Halliburton, exploring deepest Africa with David Livingstone, and going on Safari with Martin and Osa Johnson. We were enthralled with The *Last Days of Pompeii* and being with Christ at his crucifixion in *The Robe.* We laughed through Betty MacDonald's *The Egg and I* and ended with *Kon-Tiki,* an astonishing adventure of a 4,300-mile journey across the Pacific Ocean by raft.

As a family, we tried to do as much as we could together. I encouraged Tommy and Jorette to take on responsibilities and to be self-sufficient. I tried to make even the most trivial task fun for all of us. In many ways, this helped them become independent and self-directed. Tom learned to bake a pie, cinnamon rolls, and brownies before he was in junior high school. More than once, it amused the girls at the hospital to hear me give him directions over the telephone on how to make something he had taken a notion to eat. One night he wanted to make cinnamon rolls, which he did, but when I got home, they had eaten all but two—which they saved for me.

When Tom went to the National Boy Scout Jamboree in Valley Forge in 1950, he was one of the best cooks there. Jorette also loved to cook and started getting meals when she was in 6th grade. It was her way of helping out, because in good weather, I preferred to work in my flower garden rather than cook a meal. However, when she took homemaking class, her knowledge of cooking proved to be a handicap, as she thought in some ways she knew more than her teacher did!

That September, I bought a Whirlpool automatic washing machine. It cost $339.95, which was a large expenditure on my income. Up until then we had a wringer washer and rinsing tub in the basement. Jorette liked to help load the clothes into the washtub and watch them agitate in the water. After fifteen minutes, I would take each item and run it through two rollers to squeeze water out of the clothing. Each item was put through the wringer separately and the extracted wash water would fall back into the tub to be reused for the next wash load. I was afraid Jorette's fingers might be caught in the rollers, so I never allowed her to use the wringer if I was not nearby.

The automatic washing machine was so much better. Papa installed it in the kitchen and ran the water pipe underneath the floor so the wash water would run onto the lawn rather than into the septic tank. Since it was safe to operate, the children could run the Whirlpool when I was not around. We did not have a clothes dryer, but hung the clothes to dry on clotheslines in the backyard or in the basement depending upon the weather.

I had not taken a real vacation in five years, and I dreamt of getting away from the telephone and hospital responsibilities. Therefore, the children and I looked at Greyhound bus trips that were available to us. A spirit of freedom took hold of me as I looked over various itineraries. In August 1951, we left on a seven-day bus trip through New England. One of the joys of traveling by bus was meeting fellow travelers. The children made friends with everyone in our tour group and several new acquaintances wrote to us after we got home.

Jorette got bus sick on the long ride from New York City to Burlington, Vermont, so from then on, the bus driver insisted she sit in the front of the bus. The first night in a hotel, we heard a pounding on the wall. A nearby guest could not get out of her room and the manager was unable to unlock her door. Tom was in the hall observing the situation, and after a minute or two suggested that he take the pins out of the hinges. He then helped the manager do it and everything was fine. Therefore, in no time at all, Tom became the hero of the day.

During the bus ride to Portland, Tom and Jorette became acquainted with a professor from Notre Dame. Later on, when we toured the Longfellow House in Cambridge, Massachusetts, the children looked at the guest registry and wrote down the names of everyone in our tour group. From then on, they made it their business to become acquainted with each person. By the time we reached Boston and Concord, they had become friends with everyone and so it was natural to exchange addresses with each other when the tour ended. The children developed a strong attachment for Mr. Pence, who encouraged them to call him "Professor."

It was such a relief for me to get away from the hospital and from the telephone that week. I learned to close my thoughts on work when I left the hospital—except when I heard a telephone ring. Then I automatically jumped. Although the calls were more often for the children than for me, this startled reaction to the ringing of a telephone was something I could never overcome.

We had only been home two weeks when Tom and Jorette received the Professor's first two letters. His interest in them gave us a much-needed lift. Over the next few years, we all corresponded with him regularly and the result was a deep friendship. The following summer the professor took the three of us on a second trip through New England. He felt we missed too many important historic sites on the first trip, so this time he drove his car and invited us to go along. (We corresponded with the Professor for three years until we learned of his sudden death in a train accident.)

\* \* \*

Upon returning home from our first trip to New England, my mind was full of ideas for new flowerbeds and I began dividing and transplanting perennial plants. That year, our tomatoes had all blighted. However, the corn crop was plentiful, so we processed the corn to put away in our new Philco freezer. Jorette helped prepare one-half bushel of plums that we made into jam. Later we canned thirty quarts of applesauce. Most summers, we canned tomatoes, tomato juice, peaches and cherries, made pickles, and blackberry, raspberry, and strawberry jam. The shelves in the cellar supplied us with canned fruits and vegetables all year long.

Our large vegetable garden was work for all of us, but each summer, it produced abundant crops and kept our food expenses down. We all planted the seeds but Tom did most of the hoeing and weeding as well as keeping the lawn mowed. The garden was a good family activity and the children were quite proud of their efforts. When Tom and I worked together, we chatted about school and all sorts of things while Jorette prepared supper, so in essence we had perfect teamwork.

I do not recall when I became interested in raising flowers; no one in my family was flower conscious like me. To be sure, vegetables are important for the body but the beauty of flowers is just as necessary for the soul. Friends driving by our house would stop to see my lovely flowers and I frequently sent them home with seedlings to add to their gardens. I always preferred perennials but could not resist buying geraniums, marigolds, and petunias for hanging baskets.

When school resumed, I went back to working whenever I was needed. Sometimes I worked three hours, sometimes eighteen or more with an occasional day off, week in and week out. Each year the children became more involved in activities outside the home. Jorette started babysitting when she turned eleven and by the time she was a freshman in high school, she had six families who called on her quite regularly. Tom spent hours with my brother Paul who taught him about fishing, hunting, trapping, and roughing it in the outdoors. Paul was a big influence upon Tom in those years when he needed male companionship, and Tom, in turn, was the son Paul never had since he and Genevieve never had children. He was also involved in Boy Scouts and looked forward to going on camping trips. One year, the troop camped at a Scout camp behind the Pinnacle and nearly froze in -10 degree temperatures. The boys only got four hours of sleep and came home early in the morning after finding their food had frozen solid.

*Papa and Mama's 50th wedding anniversary*
*Jorette, Mildred, Papa, Tom, Mama, Paul, and Genevieve*

On January 23, 1951, Paul and I had a large dinner celebration at the Sherwood Hotel for our parents' 50$^{th}$ Wedding Anniversary. Mama's family from Albany, Papa's relatives from Greene, and longtime friends made up the three dozen guests who attended. After the dinner, the dinner guests walked to Papa and Mama's house where afternoon callers came to congratulate them and wish them well. During the afternoon, Jorette and Tom helped serve punch and wedding cake. It was a red-letter day for my parents.

\* \* \*

By the time the children were in high school, they were so busy that they went to the movies less frequently than they had when they were younger. We listened to the news and a few programs on the radio. A favorite saying of each of their teachers was, "Now do my homework even if you don't do any other," and they always had lots of homework to do. How glad I was that we did not have television to distract them.

Tom's freshman year in high school was the first time that school took on meaning for him. Previously he fooled around much of the time and frequently had detention. Jorette, on the other hand, was conscientious and took her studies very seriously. When Tom went out for football in tenth grade, he let his homework slide because football practice was so strenuous that he was too tired to do anything after supper. Only occasionally did he continue to attend Scout meetings and sometimes even skipped a Civil Air Patrol class. Tom and Jorette were very independent and seldom asked for my help except for French or spelling, so my part in guiding their thoughts was merely to suggest at times. Anyway, I wanted them to do their own thinking and use their own words.

Photography became an obsession with Tom just before our first trip to New England. It interested him more than anything else did. Once I brought an old camera magazine home from the hospital and upon reading it, he just had to subscribe to that magazine. He read everything he could find on the subject and spent every spare moment in the cellar where he set up a darkroom. He found several others kids interested in photography and before I knew it, Tom and Jorette had a small photography club meeting in our basement. Mr. Bly, the junior high science teacher, came up frequently as he knew a lot about processing film, but less work was accomplished when he was there because he acted like a big kid himself. It was not long before Tom was no longer satisfied with printing contact prints and diligently set about making an enlarger. When it did not prove satisfactory, he ordered one through the magazine. Then he spent hours working alone printing photos of our trips; he could process ten enlargements in an hour.

I will never forget what happened one autumn when I was burning the leaves in the ditch by the road. A strong wind came up and caused the fire to jump across the fire line I had made onto the property of my neighbor to the east. In no time at all, it started to sweep toward the open field. Two of the cemetery men who had just finished burning leaves in the ditch across the road came over and the three of us worked diligently to stop that fire, but it was too much for us. I had to call the fire department. Was I embarrassed! If it had gotten out of hand, it might have reached the hillside and I hate to think what would have happened.

During hunting season, Tom shot his first deer the day after Thanksgiving. He was hunting with Paul when the deer bounded into range of Paul's gun. His shot hit it in the hip. Tom followed the trail of blood and shortly afterwards when the deer came into view, he shot the deer right through the head. It was a four pointer and weighed 140 pounds. When the hunters returned home, they were all smiles. Tom was the envy of all the boys in school on Monday.

We never seriously thought about having a television set until 1953 when I came across a deep plot underfoot by my children. Tom and Jorette planned to draw their money out of the bank to buy one for me for my birthday so I would not mind staying at home alone so much. I could not see them spend what little money they had saved, so I bought a 17-inch cabinet model Zenith TV set for $292. Since it was *Greene Days*, Greene Radio and Television offered a 10% discount that paid for the installation and the aerial. The reception was very good on Channel 12. The picture was in black and white in the fifties, as color television did not become popular until the late sixties. Our favorite shows quickly became *I Love Lucy, Our Miss Brooks, Arthur Godfrey and Friends, What's My Line,* and *Dragnet.*

* * *

When Tom was in his junior year, an event happened that really shook me to the core. Tom had gone over to David Bartlett's home to hang out for the day. That afternoon, I received a phone call from the Greene Emergency Squad telling me that Tom, Dave, and Bobby Hunter had taken a canoe down the Genegantslet Creek thinking how much fun it would be navigating the raging flood waters. For some reason, they neglected to consider the danger. The canoe capsized before reaching the Chenango River, tossing the boys into the turbulent water. David and Bobby managed to reach a small island while Tom caught hold of a tree. Their cries attracted the attention of Melvin Bates who ran to get his horse. He was able to reach the two boys on horseback and bring them to safety just as the Emergency Squad arrived. With the squad boat, four squad members rescued Tom who was fighting to keep his hold on the tree. Only God's grace put someone on the scene that had the courage to enter the swift current to rescue the boys. My undying gratitude went out to the heroic actions of the Emergency Squad, who saved Tom from drowning. The boys' irresponsibility could very well have ended in disaster. The event was on TV as well as on the radio news.

A week later, I had an operation on my right shoulder and was a patient in the Binghamton City Hospital for a few days. While I was hospitalized, the children took it upon themselves to varnish the living room and dining room furniture, paint the radiators, the furniture in Jorette's room and the porch glider. I was very amazed how much they accomplished and how well everything was done.

During the last two years of high school, Tom and Jorette were seldom home for long. They became absorbed in their own interests and lived in a world of their own filled with numerous activities and friends. Tom was involved in

Civil Air Patrol, wrestling, cleaning the movie theater or the church, hunting during deer season, and trapping during the winter. One winter he and Bobby Hunter trapped sixty-two muskrats that they eventually sold for their fur. Jorette began working at the Moore Memorial Library in addition to babysitting, being head color guard in the band, on the archery team, in Footlights Society, and substituting at the theater making popcorn or selling tickets. In addition to their activities, they did homework, helped around home, and led an active social life. They were the busiest children I ever saw.

Life was never dull around our house with the children's friends coming and going. The following is an entry from my diary of a typical day in our lives:

> *Jan. 2, 1952—worked at the hospital 9–3, bought groceries on my walk home—Back to the hospital from 8–10 p.m. for a delivery. Jo went to Binghamton with Phyllis Waldon to buy some long socks (the latest fad). She was home by 5:30 and went to the movies with Sally Henninge at 7 p.m. Tom escorted her through the cemetery because of the rabid fox scare. Tom and Bobby Hunter took up their mink traps this a.m., then he went skating all afternoon with Dave Bartlett. Was home by 6 p.m. After supper, he developed pictures in the cellar all evening. After a snack all were in bed by midnight.*

After Tom got his driver's license and I had a learner's permit, the children thought I needed a car, especially when it looked hopeful that I might learn how to drive. My parents took Tom and me to look at used cars and I was fortunate to find a reasonably priced green 1950 Ford Tudor car for $950. A month later, we three took a six-day trip to Montreal and Quebec with Tom driving. Tom was a good driver and I had confidence in him, which was more than I could say for myself. When my learner's permit expired, I did not renew it because Papa was so nervous when he took me out to drive that I decided to skip the whole thing. I had never really wanted to drive and believed, "One does not miss what one never had." Both children turned out to be good drivers and were happy to chauffeur me back and forth to work while they were living at home. After Tom got his license, it was wonderful to be driven to work at 6:45 in the morning and see him waiting to take me home when I finished work. If it was raining or snowing, I appreciated the ride twice as much.

As Tom's senior year approached, he debated upon whether to go to college or go to work. Of course, I wanted both of my children to get an education and had always encouraged them to do so. After looking into various career opportunities, he became interested in the merchant marines. He thought marine transportation sounded like an interesting career and selected the New York State Maritime College at Fort Schuyler to be his first choice. Tom sent in his application and within three weeks received an invitation to appear for an interview and tour the campus.

Mama and I accompanied Tom to New York City and planned to spend the day going into the city once we had seen Tom safely at Fort Schuyler, but it was so windy and cold that we lost all desire to walk to the closest bus stop. Therefore, we waited in our car, walked about, and talked with other parents while Tom took a battery of exams during the morning. At noon, a cadet escorted him to lunch and on a tour of inspection of the campus. The cadet made no bones about the rigid discipline and six hours of homework every night, and that cadets must wear full uniforms at all times and were not allowed to leave the post wearing civilian clothes.

Before we left for home, Tom had a personal interview before an admissions board. He felt he had handled the interview very well. Overall, Tom was very impressed and doubted he would have a problem with the discipline or the amount of homework. Having worked in military hospitals, I wondered how Tom would adapt to being closely supervised at all times. However, he felt it was a good school and was intrigued with the opportunity to travel on the college's training ship each summer while getting hands-on experience in leadership and the maritime industry.

To me, the academy looked like all work and no play and military to the nth degree. Except for the fort itself, all other buildings were of frame barracks type construction. I myself, would choose a different sort of institution of learning—a larger one with fine old buildings and a lovely campus—something to appeal to my esthetic sense—as well as a place with tradition. Each to his own choice however, and I had no intention to cast one shadow of discouragement on Tom's choice.

A week after his interview, Tom received a letter ordering him to report for his physical exam at the New York Recruiting Office in just five days. We were in a dither, as he had to have all necessary dental work done before reporting. One of the local dentists squeezed Tom in for five necessary fillings, so he was all set to go back to New York for the necessary medical tests. Ten days later, Fort Schuyler accepted him on all counts. These were exciting days for all of us.

In the second semester of Jorette's junior year, she came home from school all excited one day. She announced she had a new job: counting money in the cafeteria during one period each day. Not long afterward, Mr. Beebe, the school principal, asked her if she would be interested in working more hours at the public library. She had started working there on Saturday mornings and now Mrs. Whitaker, the librarian, wanted her to work additional hours if the school thought it would not interfere with her studies. It seems that everyone was so good to us. The kindness of people just overwhelmed me at times.

Jorette was very enthusiastic about working in the public library. Her first big task was helping Mrs. Whitaker inventory the book collection. She enjoyed working at the circulation desk and quickly learned the interests of frequent library patrons. It was not long before she began talking about studying to be a librarian.

My work at the hospital kept me busier than ever when Tom and Jorette were in their senior years. There was often a patient in nearly every room on each floor. Many times, I ended up working fourteen-hour days rather than my usual day of 6:30 a.m. to 4 p.m. The main benefit was a larger paycheck at a time when looming before me was the expense of Tom's year-round education. After Tom was born, I took out a policy with Investor's Syndicate for this specific purpose. I was faithful except for two years when I was financially unable to make payments, thus delaying its maturity. When Jorette's time for college comes, I believed that by cutting back on household expenses, my salary should cover her.

Over the years, I have had to forego many of what people call the simplest necessities and have learned to do without. I taught the children to weigh each purchase carefully: was it a need or a want? In order to have what I felt were the most important things, we had to make sacrifices of the lesser. I am now very thankful that I have been able to earn enough to support the three of us and that both Tom and Jorette were able to find jobs as soon as they were old enough to get working papers. With the good Lord's help, I was able to swing both college educations.

* * *

To celebrate Tom graduating, the three of us went on our last vacation together. He drove us to Washington, DC, where we spent three days visiting the Capitol, seeing the monuments, and exploring museums. It was a wonderful time for us. All too soon, the graduation, long anticipated, had come and gone. It was a joyous occasion for Tom and his girlfriend, Kay McNulty, and all their friends, but it was the opposite for me. As I sat home alone after all the festivities, I felt content yet sad and even a bit stunned, for these eighteen years had gone unbelievably fast. Looking back, I see years of happiness and loneliness divided like sunshine and rain. For what I have and have had, I am thankful, and feel, I am far more fortunate than many.

Tom's girlfriend began her college career at Cortland State Teachers College immediately following graduation. Kay's goal was to go to college the year round and get her degree in three years. She was ambitious and a born organizer. Tom and Kay started dating in their junior year and her home was a second home to him.

In July, Tom received a letter from the University of the State of New York saying he was eligible for a State Scholarship. Tom and I were overjoyed! The scholarship totaled $1,400 to be paid in two $175 installments directly to the college each year. That was a tremendous help to me. It was like a miracle! Day after day, I would marvel at how good the Lord is to us. The Greene Central School faculty was also very happy about Tom's scholarship, as he was the first boy to get one in years, and it was the first time our school ever received three of the ten scholarships awarded to each county.

One day, when Jorette and I were shopping in Binghamton, we decided to look at cars, because the one we had was a constant headache with one problem after another. I never thought we would buy one that day, but we found a 1953 Nash Rambler—Tudor gray and red—and we immediately fell in love with it. It was equipped with everything but overdrive and even had seats that tilted way down. It cost $1,695 less $400 for the trade-in allowance on our car. We kept it a secret from my parents because we wanted to surprise them when we drove it home a few days later. So now, I may have to work extra to support this new vehicle. I hoped it would not have the mechanical problems we had with the Ford.

I thought life would be quieter once Tom left for college, but that was not the case. Jorette's senior year seemed busier than Tom's once she became sole operator of the car. We made several trips to Fort Schuyler to attend special events. On Visitor's Day, Tom's girlfriend, Kay McNulty, went with us to see the cadets' official dress review. Tom hitchhiked home at least twice a month, frequently bringing a friend with him. After one year at Fort Schuyler, Tom decided the military lifestyle was not for him and transferred to Harpur College in Binghamton to study geology.

Jorette started looking at colleges in New York State that had a library science major, so we drove to Geneseo State Teacher's College to see if their program would be a good fit for her. We both liked the size of the campus and its location, and it was within my financial means. My salary in 1954 was $2,697.84.[6]

* * *

During the summer of 1955, I took a leave of absence from the hospital. Jorette suggested that she and I drive to the West Coast as soon as she graduated and be back shortly before leaving for college in September. For years, I worked and sacrificed, never taking more than a week off for a vacation, so I decided it was time to do things differently and go on a trip we would never forget. Jorette saved her money from her library and theatre jobs for expenses she would incur on the trip and was eager to pay her share of expenses. I never expected to be fortunate enough to go on a long automobile trip and had not dared let my thoughts dwell on it too much because it seemed so improbable. Dreams, dreams, but, poignantly lovely ones! I did all the planning of places to go and people to see and Jorette did all the driving. We traveled through twenty-two states, over 10,000 miles and visited many national parks and places of historic interest. What a wonderful time we had sightseeing, visiting old friends from my years in nursing training and first cousins who had moved to Arizona and California.. We will never forget driving through New Mexico and Arizona. The temperature was 118 degrees and it was so hot in the car we could barely stand it. When we stopped for gas, an attendant suggested we buy a large chunk of dry ice and place it under the vent. The incoming air would make us feel cooler as the dry ice evaporated. Well, we had never heard of such a thing, but we tried it and it helped.[7]

When we arrived in Los Angeles, Jorette met her father for the first time in nearly twelve years. She spent a few days with Jimmy and his wife Olivine and I stayed with a cousin who had moved to L.A. from Albany. It was an awkward situation for Jorette and Jimmy but at last, she had an

---

[6] www.ssa.gov the average annual salary in 1954 was $3,155.54

[7] The first affordable heating and air-conditioning system in cars was introduced in 1954. By 1960, about 20% of American cars had air-conditioning. http://en.wikipedia.org/wiki/Air_conditioning

opportunity to get to know her father. Then we drove to Seattle, Washington, to meet Jimmy's mother, Cora Macquarrie, and her children by a second marriage. It was so exhilarating to connect personalities with names and learn about Jimmy's side of the family. I had named Jorette after her grandmother, so imagine our surprise when we learned her maiden name was Cora Jarrett rather than Cora Jorette.

We had so many interesting experiences on our Western trip. Sometimes we stayed at motels or cabins, camped in a tent at national or state parks, or stayed with friends and family. We often picked up hitchhikers. I recall several of them vividly—a young Indian man who rode with us for forty miles and barely uttered a word of English. Another time, we befriended an interesting 25-year-old man who was hitching around the country and he stuck with us for three days. When we stayed in our motel, he slept on the ground next to our car. In the morning, we allowed him to shower in our room while we ate breakfast in a cafe. We gave him any food we did not eat. Having an extra person to talk to in the car made the journey much more interesting as we drove across those wide open spaces in the West.

One of the best parts of traveling, no matter how pleasant, is getting home. No valley is lovelier than our Chenango, no village any prettier and surely no folks any friendlier. As soon as the door was unlocked, Jorette and I set out to look around the yard at our flowerbeds and then call friends to tell them we were home. When I returned to the hospital, work had piled up in my absence and it took me days to catch up. Everyone greeted me so enthusiastically that I determined to get away more often, if possible. I never thought they would miss me as much as they did in the two months I was away. Maybe it is natural to feel that way when one is too close to things for too long. At that time, I had been superintendent of the hospital for nine years.

Looking back, I can see how the Lord provided for us every step of the way. Tom was janitor in our church and at the Greene Theatre and later worked in the A&P Store on Genesee Street plus finding other odd jobs in the summer. Jorette babysat, worked in the school cafeteria, the Moore

Memorial Library, and the theatre. They developed a strong work ethic and learned self-discipline in managing money—always saving a portion of their earnings. They paid for the gasoline for the car and never asked for an allowance after they earned their own money. Neither Tom nor Jorette had class rings or went on class trips, but there was never one complaint about those things.

Ours was definitely not the "average American family" as we did not have a TV until 1953 or a car until later that year when Tom got his driver's license. Nevertheless, we took a family vacation each summer, going on short trips to New England, Niagara Falls, New York City, Quebec, and Washington, DC. The children were well adjusted, popular, and had their priorities in order. Life was good and I was very proud of my family.

# Chapter 11

## On Call 24/7 at the Greene Hospital

*I don't know what your destiny will be,
but one thing I know: the only ones among you
who will be really happy are those who will
have sought and found how to serve.*
—Albert Schweitzer

Greene did not have a hospital when I was growing up. It was not until 1939 that Dr. Carl Meacham and Dr. Charles Chapin conceived the idea of converting Bessie Turner's nursing home at 39 North Canal Street into a small private hospital. Up until then, a doctor frequently performed emergency operations on a kitchen table and delivered babies at home.

The Turner Hospital was quite a help to the community. It specialized in maternity care and chronic illnesses requiring hospitalization. In 1942, Alvan and Linn Hill bought the hospital and remodeled the building to a nineteen-bed capacity. The Hill brothers opened the hospital on January 1, 1943, under the name of the Greene Hospital. Catherine Race, RN, was its first superintendent and Maude Mosher, RN, succeeded her. In 1946, I became the third superintendent and ended up working there the entire eighteen years that the hospital remained in operation.

The hospital was originally a two-story house enlarged to accommodate eighteen patients and six infants. It had the necessary exits, stairways, and elevator to meet fire regulations. The first floor was set aside for maternity care, an office, and the kitchen. On the second floor, there were private and semi-private rooms for medical and surgical patients and an operating room.

*The Greene Hospital*

Working in a small-town hospital was different from other hospital nursing I had done. This small community hospital had limited equipment, but our patients never lacked for good medical care. The small staff knew most of the patients, their families, and even their acquaintances. We cared about each individual, those who were injured and dying, the mothers who were about to deliver their new babies, the victims of accidents, and patients sick with pneumonia and other illnesses. We would often sit by a bedside during the night offering hope and encouragement. I learned that people in a small community lean on you and I knew that this was indeed my calling.

I quickly found that being hospital superintendent, working a shift, and filling in when one of our small staff was ill was indeed challenging and demanding. My administrative duties included hiring staff, working closely with the physicians to ensure the best patient care, reporting any changes in patients' status to the doctors, and keeping accurate records in accordance with state standards. My responsibilities were never-ending when it came to scheduling the nursing staff, making out paychecks on the first and fifteenth day of each month, ordering hospital supplies, and doing other necessary bookkeeping. Milly Auwarter (Alvan Hill's daughter) was the accountant and came in once a month to do the monthly financial reports.

For many years, I was the only RN and on call twenty-four hours a day. The help were licensed practical nurses. When I was not on duty and an emergency came in, the first thing the doctors asked was "Where's Mildred?" When the LPN on duty notified the doctor that a maternity case had come in, he would respond, "Call Mildred." It was a blessed day for me when we found an RN to work the night shift and to relieve me at other times of many lengthy maternity vigils.

Approximately 1,100 babies were born at the hospital during the years I was superintendent. The maternity floor included a labor room, delivery room, patient rooms, and a nursery. The waiting room for expectant fathers was opposite my office, just a few steps from the labor room. In those days, fathers-to-be did not enter the delivery room so I got to know some patients' husbands quite well as almost ten percent of families had four or more children back then.

The baby boom began in 1945 after the end of WWII when millions of veterans returned home, got married, and started families. It reached its peak in the late 1950s when the number of children born to an average woman began to decline. Sometimes a new mother looked forward to staying a week to ten days in the hospital to "get off her feet" and rest up before going home to her other small children. Most expectant mothers from our area elected to have their babies locally rather than drive to a larger hospital in Binghamton or Johnson City, so we took our role in the life of the community very seriously as the maternity ward was the heart of the hospital.

About the same time that I became superintendent of the Greene Hospital in 1946, Drs. Everett and Erwin Centerwall set up practice. They, along with Dr. Charles Chapin and Dr. Newton Brachin, used the hospital for their patients. The Centerwall brothers arranged for surgeons from Binghamton to come to perform needed surgery, with the local doctor administering the anesthetic. In most cases, the local doctors were able to perform appendectomies and tonsillectomies. All of our doctors delivered babies.

There was a tonsil clinic at the hospital on July 11, just three months after I started working full time. Children with enlarged or infected tonsils had the opportunity to have their tonsils removed. The surgery took place in the operating room on the second floor. After each child was fully awake from the ether and doing well, a nurse gave ice cream to each one of them to sooth their throat before they were sent home. Jorette was the only child to stay overnight in the hospital due to my being on duty; the others stayed only a few hours.

When I first started working at the hospital, my home phone was a party line. After we moved into our new house in 1947, the Hill Brothers insisted I have a private line installed to make sure I would be immediately accessible. In the next eight years while Tom and Jorette were still in school, there were times when I practically ran my home by telephone. It always seemed that whenever I planned a family holiday meal, I would be called away in the midst of it. It was exasperating but funny! All we could do was laugh about it.

We lived a mile from the hospital and I walked to and from work. Whenever I was called in for an emergency, I would take a cab if one was available, or sometimes an ambulance would come for me, occasionally the hearse, and often a patient's husband. The attending doctor frequently drove me home afterward. For a brief time, Richard Mills, the owner of the Sherwood Hotel, had a taxi service, so I could usually get a ride until 1 a.m. when the taproom closed. The bartender always managed to find someone to drive Mrs. Cochrane to the hospital when Mr. Mills was unavailable.

One night a man known to be a drunkard showed up at my doorstep and drove me to the hospital. He reeked from alcohol. That was the first time I was even the least bit nervous. When I reached the hospital, I laughingly told Dr. Centerwall and the nurse on duty about it and said, "Now I know I've had all the drunks in town drive me down here." However, they did not think it was funny. "Now see here, Mildred, you've just got to get yourself a car," said Dr. C. I replied, "Do you think I'd be safer driving than riding with them?" His answer was most emphatic, "Yes, I do!" Reluctantly, I promised that I would sign up for driver's training as soon as the school purchased a dual-control car. In April of 1952, I finally took a driver's training course, but I never took the driver's test. I was convinced that people were much safer on the road without me driving.

Hiring nurses was difficult those first few years. I was on the lookout for any new nurse who moved to Greene. When I first started working at the hospital, I was the only RN working there. By the summer of 1952, the situation had changed and we had RNs on all shifts except for the one relief nurse. Sometimes our hospital beds were nearly all occupied and scheduling help became challenging. However, when the patient load was light the hospital ran behind financially. When that happened it was natural to worry about whether the owners would consider it worthwhile to keep the hospital open.

\* \* \*

The Greene Hospital was a pleasant place to work and the employees took as much interest in it as in their own homes. When the patient load was slack, we might mend or even paint furniture and woodwork. If the cleaning woman failed to show up for work, we did her work as well. Despite all this, the only reason any employee left during my first six years was that she either moved away or had a baby. We were like a family unit, helping each other, working overtime, and exchanging shifts to keep everyone happy. Whenever anything unpleasant came up, I took on the role of peacemaker.

Until the early fifties we were busy most of the time and frequently had to put up extra beds in the waiting room, hall, and even in the operating room. However, with the widespread use of penicillin most people stayed at home unless they had hospital insurance or were seriously ill. Doctors sent maternity patients home in four or five days because they now allowed new mothers out of bed on the second day, and the Binghamton surgeon contracted to do our operating had so much work that he simply could no longer find the time to come to Greene. Consequently, our patients began going to Binghamton or Norwich hospital for major surgery and bone work. For these reasons and others, the hospital began to run behind financially.

It was over five years before I took my first vacation. That summer I finally rebelled. I was exhausted and felt that I was merely a slave to the hospital. I decided that my children should come first. They were fourteen and fifteen and at an age where I should be with them, for all too soon they would be out of high school and gone. The thought made me panicky. Therefore, during their summer vacation I only took night calls and went in to do the office work. I handled all other hospital business over the telephone. Then to get away from that phone, we took a weeklong bus trip through New England. My desire was that Tom and Jorette should learn about people and places that have made their imprint on history. I wanted them to become familiar with hotels, restaurants, and bus stations to make it easier for the day when they would be leaving home and doing things on their own. We had taken a few short trips to New York City, Niagara Falls, and other places in New York State with Mama and Papa, but our travels were limited due to my inability to drive a car.

* * *

Each day brought challenges to our small staff. I will never forget the caring bedside manner each nurse showed to a local man who had a freak accident one cold January. It seems he stepped outside his house one evening and apparently slipped off the back steps and pitched head foremost onto the ice, cutting his forehead and knocking him out. No one knew how long he lay there. He was brought into the hospital just before I got there at 11 p.m. His clothing was completely soaked through from the icy water and his limbs rigid. Had it been colder that night, he would have frozen to death. This was the first time I had seen such a bad case of exposure. It took all night to thaw him out and all the next day for him to regain any feeling. His hands were paralyzed—and only after ten days, did he begin to feed himself and hold onto things.

That same winter, the night nurse was ill for two weeks so I began taking her place. Whenever I worked on the night shift and had a spare moment I would busy myself by straightening up the medicine cabinet, arranging the stacks of linen just so, rearranging magazines in the waiting rooms, and I never went into a patient's room without tidying it up. Only once during those two weeks was it necessary for me to go on duty early and work over into the next day because of a maternity case. Then I worked without a break for nineteen hours—from 11 p.m. Wednesday to 6 p.m. on Thursday. Fortunately, I had not scheduled myself to work Thursday night as that was the night the relief always worked. A difficult maternity case involving twins kept me on duty all that day. One was born naturally at 11:30 a.m., the second at 4:40 p.m. Dr. Brachin called in a surgeon from Norwich to perform a high forceps delivery for the second baby. The babies weighed 7lb. 2 oz. and 7lb. 1½ oz., respectively. These babies were the young mother's fifth delivery. She wanted a girl desperately but got two more boys! Never have we had a more hysterical patient, or one who said she hated boys. She would not own them. Well, naturally, we needed to watch her closely and every nurse put in overtime for several days. The beautiful baby boys looked just alike except one was blond and the other brunette. In the end, she reconciled to having two more boys and everything turned out happily after all.

The difference between our hospital and city hospitals concerning maternity care was that we did no "forced" labors. Our doctors took time to let nature take its course. They did not rush their patients through labor and it was seldom necessary to resort to forceps. In the hundreds of deliveries in which I assisted, the majority of births were normal deliveries. There were no infections and no scarred babies; we were proud of our fine record and the care each mother and infant received during the time they spent with us.

Over the years, it was a common occurrence to receive a phone call late at night and for me to make a quick dash to the hospital. One particular Sunday night the nurse on duty sent a visitor up with his truck for me as the night taxi was no longer available. It was just luck that he was visiting his mother at that hour as she had taken a turn for the worse. The maternity patient's husband could not pick me up because they lived close enough to walk to the hospital, which they chose to do. Well when I walked in and saw her, I knew that I had to step lively. I quickly picked up the phone to call Dr. Centerwall and told him to come right over, but "right over" became ten minutes later. In the meantime, I had to deliver the baby and cut the cord wound tightly around the baby's neck. Dr. Centerwall found the three of us waiting for him when he arrived. I could never understand why this patient walked those two blocks knowing how fast she had delivered her previous babies. Dr. Centerwall drove me home and I was in bed exactly one hour later. This was not the first or last time I would deliver a baby by myself. I wish I had kept count of how many times the baby arrived before the doctor.

I seldom talked about my work to anyone not of the medical profession. This was to keep from thinking about the hospital when I was at home. When the children asked me about work I would recount an interesting event or two, but I tried to make them my priority when I left the hospital. I determined that I would not neglect my interest in my children or my parents and in reading and gardening.

It became easier for me to put in longer hours at the hospital once the children were in high school. When the influenza epidemic forced the school to close for a week in February 1953, I worked for three weeks without a day off. I worked alternate shifts due to either sickness of the nurses or of their families. Fortunately, I escaped being ill with the flu, but struggled along with a miserable cold. The difficulties of juggling work and family surfaced in times like this, but I believed that with the help of God *you do what you have to do.*

When the hospital was full of patients, I would go in two hours earlier each morning and work later than usual to get all my work done. I never minded the hours spent nursing but often pushed myself to the limits to get the office work done. We frequently had a run of sick patients who needed constant attention, as well as a maternity case, which meant added stress and constant running up and down stairs. To watch a maternity patient from the time she comes in until she delivers is a job by itself *and* so is taking care of two floors of patients and babies. Together it could be overwhelming for only one nurse, so from time to time I was called to find a relief nurse to help out.

Early in 1950, the Hill Brothers voiced their concern about the hospital's precarious financial situation. They were sustaining a deficit each year and covering the debt themselves. Fearing that Alvan or Linn Hill would give up, a group of citizens organized a Hospital Association to acquire funds to make up the annual deficit and to improve facilities at the hospital with a long-range plan for a new hospital. The high school band held concerts to raise money and individual contributions were forthcoming.

One of the most successful fundraisers was the Grand Old Ball. Burr Harrington, a local dance instructor, produced and directed four balls (1950–1953). The people involved had to go to rehearsals to practice the Grand March which was the highlight of each dance. According to Mr. Harrington, "This was unlike anything ever presented before in Greene." Those of us who attended will never forget it. People talked about the Grand Old Ball for months and eagerly looked forward to the next year.

At one of the dances, I found it quite amusing to have one of Greene's eligible bachelors dance every dance with me from the moment he spotted me coming in the door with Tom and Jorette. I enjoyed it quite as much as I did the curious looks on the faces of those sitting in the balcony until it came time to go home and he wanted to drive us home. There I drew the line and we rode home with neighbors. I knew the town would buzz enough thinking we came with him—and it did.

Then, in May 1953, Alvan Hill announced that the hospital would close on June 1. The deficit for the hospital for the previous year was $7,000. Each year the Hill brothers covered the loss, but could no longer do so. Some reasons for the deficits were unpaid patient bills, the cost of three registered nurses and other expenses involved in running the hospital. At that time, the hospital needed to clear $66 per day in order to break even, which necessitated caring for an average of six patients a day. In summer months, the patient load occasionally dropped to half that number. To make matters worse, the New York State Social Welfare Department was constantly demanding costly renovations to comply with changes in regulations.

Once again, there was a flurry of activity to save the hospital and members of the community sprang into action. Many organizations agreed to refurbish a room. The Rotary Club was the first to choose a room and the men painted the ceiling, walls, woodwork, varnished the floor, bought Venetian blinds, sanded and varnished chairs, and had slipcovers made. Then the Baptist Church social group did the same for the next largest room, followed by the Business and Professional Women who purchased new spreads and made drapes for the windows. The Methodist Church refurbished another room and members of the Congregational Church painted the nursery, bought blinds, and made drapes for seven windows. The Smithville Valley Grange renovated and painted another room. There were droves of people working around the patients evening after evening. Other organizations and individuals followed suit. It seemed that I was in constant conference with various individuals about colors, materials, needs, and suggestions. I hardly expected them to do anything more than painting and varnishing to spruce up the rooms. The results were outstanding and were we delighted! We took all the visitors around to show them the change. The outpouring of time and talent was a blessing. Local merchants gave all the materials at cost. When completed, the Raymond Corporation bought eight new mattresses, the Grange purchased over-the-bed tables, and the community continued to raise money to keep the hospital afloat. This wonderful outpouring of community spirit makes Greene a very special place to live.

Over the years, the *Chenango American* published many articles about the valiant attempt of the community to keep the hospital going. Amid the uncertainty of the hospital's survival, our staff never wavered, responding to every emergency and providing excellent care of our patients. What we did, we did well, and our community supported us all the way. Many patients told me they received better care here than in a large hospital, but I think that is due to the personal gestures like shopping for patients, reading their mail to them, and showing concern and understanding by visiting with them, plus other acts of *kindness* that met their emotional needs as well as their physical needs.

In twenty years, the hospital staff dealt with many automobile accidents. One evening during the first week of January in 1954, there was a bad accident just south of the village. A car going south on Route 12 attempted to pass another and ran head on into a northbound bus. The driver was killed outright. His five passengers sustained broken limbs and terrible lacerations and a girl suffered the loss of an eye. Only one bus passenger suffered major injuries. The emergency squad rushed the victims to our hospital. Just as I arrived to help out, the second stretcher was being carried in, followed by four others in quick succession. The operating room and hall were full of bloody, groaning victims. Two doctors, two nurses, and the emergency squad worked as fast as we could go for the next two and one-half hours, giving emergency treatment, applying splints, and sewing up minor cuts in preparation to send the accident victims to Binghamton for care by specialists. We later learned that a second bus picked up the passengers and sped toward Utica, unloading them at various towns where each received the necessary medical care.

Our small staff was like a family and I cannot praise nearly enough everyone that I worked with over the years. They were the finest, most devoted people I had ever worked with. Nothing was ever too much for our nurses such as Helen Hunter, Sophie Sawyer, Marion Henninge, Anna Coddington, Doris Blakeslee, Wilma Thurber, Jeanette Shafer, Rachel Eckert and Phyllis Auwarter, and cooks Edythe Rounds and Faye Pangburn, and housekeepers Bessie Burgess and Dorothy Rhodes plus others who helped out whenever needed.

*The hospital staff celebrates Marion Henninge's retirement – 1961*
*Marion (on right) and daughter Sally (on left)*

Each person on our hospital staff was conscientious and considerate. Many times different nurses helped me out of a tight spot. When difficult situations arose, all of them had me to call on to help them. However, when I worked a shift, there was no one to call, unless one of them came back—and they knew I would never call them unless I was desperate. When something out of the ordinary happened during the night, such as a patient falling out of bed or one becoming unmanageable, several of our nurses lived close enough to the hospital to enlist the help of her husband.

In July 1962, an ill-fated step caused me to fall and sustain four fractures in my ankle. I spent eleven days in the

Norwich Hospital in great pain before I could be transferred to the Greene Hospital. There I could oversee the activities, do some office work, and work on historical records. One afternoon I prepared one-half bushel of beans for our cook, Mrs. Rounds. Another morning, the nurse on duty could not come to work and we were desperate until I found Betty Rutherford who had never worked for us on days and only two or three times at night. Well, it could not have been a busier day! She had an admission and a discharge, a death, a circumcision, a patient who could only get up with the aid of a Hoyer Lift, a senile patient confined to her room by a gate across her doorway, and a semi-paralytic who was difficult to get out of bed because of a fractured arm—with me to direct, advise, hop around on crutches and help in any way I could. Marcia Brown, a high-school aide, was a lifesaver, and her presence helped us keep our sanity. I spent the next fifteen days as a patient in the hospital, except for one evening when Tom took me to a hospital meeting after carrying me down the stairs to his car.

The annual hospital inspection by the State Department of Social Welfare was one we all dreaded. Not one thing was overlooked including records, procedures, policies, scheduling, licenses, finances, and compliance with various codes and regulations. It was my responsibility to spend the entire time with the inspector, answering all her questions as she scrutinized each room, attic and basement, checking each fire extinguisher as she proceeded. By the time the inspection was completed, there was nothing she did not know—and I was numb from answering all her questions. She dwelled mostly on the flaws, hardly noticing improvements. Each year a new inspector sees different things. Fire regulations in particular grew stiffer and stiffer.

Each year it became more and more apparent that New York State intended to close all small town hospitals and the end of ours was in sight. Due to the support of the community, our hospital had been able to comply with the demands of the state, keeping the hospital in operation from 1953 to 1964. There had been untold meetings concerning the future of health care services in Greene, but, in December of 1962, the New York State Welfare Department made a new ruling that became the death knell of our hospital. The ultimatum said the old hospital had to have two fire exits from the second floor and a new fireproof elevator or build a new hospital. The state agreed to allow the hospital to continue operating while plans were drawn up for a new facility. That year, we had admitted only forty maternity patients. The following December we were compelled to shut down all maternity services so bedridden patients could be moved to the first floor. Janet Leigh Barton, the daughter of Doris and Jim Barton, was the last baby to be born in the hospital on January 27, 1963. The hospital stayed in operation until it was forced to close its doors forever on March 7, 1964. The following account is from my 1964 diary.

\* \* \*

*March 3—I walked down to the hospital for the 3 to 11 shift. I didn't have a moment to look over the stack of hospital mail until after 4 o'clock and then I opened a letter from the State Social Welfare Commissioner at Albany stating that our hospital was to close its doors immediately — as soon as possible. At last it has come! For two years, our town has been fighting to keep our little hospital. However, the State is closing these small institutions as fast as they can and two nursing homes in this area closed this past fall. We cannot meet their impossible demands. Well, I called Richard Thurber immediately and he came right up for the letter. He called Fred Rosekrans, Syracuse Social Welfare Dept., the doctors, etc., and set up a special meeting for to-morrow. None of us who knew about this slept very much this night.*

*March 4—Milly Auwarter stopped for me and we went down to the Raymond Manor for a special hospital meeting. The whole board was there being served coffee. Well, many things were discussed during the lively one and one-half hour meeting. Our patients at the hospital will have to be moved by 3:00 p.m. on Saturday. The decision was quite a blow to each person. I stopped and told my folks and Jorette, and then went back to the hospital for the night. I did not do much more than talk to Edythe Rounds, Berdina Manwarren, Anna Coddington (Coddy), Rachel Eckert, and a little later, Joanne Phelps. Coddy and I stripped all the upstairs beds.*

*March 5—I worked 8–2:30 just doing office work, filing things away, and generally straightening up. I was emotionally exhausted.*

*March 7—I hated to see this day arrive. Our last two patients, Alice Thomas and May Walker were transferred to nursing homes this morning. I spent the rest of the day straightening up, washing all the rubber sheets, ironing dresser covers, cleaning, doing final office work, etc. Milly and Fred Auwarter were here to fix locks on the doors, close the garage, turn out exit lights, and do all the things necessary in closing a hospital. Mrs. Rounds got dinner for us. Ben came for her and her things and it was 5:30 by the time she got away. Then I had a sandwich and glass of juice and Jorette came for me about six o'clock and took me home. After that eleven-hour session, I was so worn out that I took a two-hour nap.*

*March 10—I went down to the hospital to get the linen ready for the laundryman and I had just finished when he came at ten o'clock. Then Milly came and the two of us spent a busy day. I was alone in the afternoon and when I got ready to leave, I could not get the door locked so had to call Jerry Alderman to come up. He could not lock it either, so I called Fred Auwarter. He said Mrs. Rounds had told him the special trick about it on Saturday. So, it was very easy after all.*

*March 11—Mayor Evans came up to my house to get a hospital key so he could put a sign in the hospital window about emergencies.*

*March 20—Milly Auwarter and I inventoried every-*
*thing in the hospital and sorted out drugs and instru-*
*ments for the doctors. My job was over after eighteen*
*years of service to the hospital and the people of*
*Greene.*

For more than ten years, Greene had fought hard to
keep the hospital running but to no avail. For twenty-two
years, the hospital had provided excellent care to several
generations of local residents, dealt with numerous diseases,
performed deliveries and some surgeries, set bones, and
took time to listen to patients. Its closing was the end of an
era.[8]

---

[8] Eventually the property was sold to Alfred E. Turner who completely
remodeled the building into an apartment house.

# Chapter 12

## Celebrate Family

*The happiest moments of my life
have been the few which I have passed
at home in the bosom of my family.*
—Thomas Jefferson

When Jorette left for college, I thought I would find myself alone, but such was not the case. Tom left Ft. Schuyler, returned home, and enrolled at Harpur College, and he and Kay McNulty became engaged. I decided it was time for me to pursue an outside interest and so I began to delve into the history of the English family. My parents encouraged me and we started visiting old cemeteries to locate family burial sites in order to assemble Papa's family genealogy. Although I started looking into the past, my life remained rooted in the present. In fifty-plus years, I had learned to accept change in my life and greet each change as a new adventure.

My children started having new adventures that often involved me. At the end of Jorette's sophomore year at Geneseo State Teachers College, she was selected to go abroad with the Experiment in International Living as Geneseo's first College Ambassador. During the summer vacation, she traveled to Vienna, Austria, where she lived with a local family for a month. The second month, she traveled with nine other Americans visiting cities in northern Italy, Germany, Holland, and Prague, Czechoslovakia. Certainly, this was a new experience for her as well as a new challenge speaking to various organizations upon her return to campus. Jorette and I took the train to New Jersey and I returned alone after she sailed from Hoboken on the S.S. *Waterman*.

A month later, I accompanied Tom in his Volkswagen to the Dubois Science Camp in Wyoming. As soon as we arrived, I caught a bus to Jackson Hole to do some sightseeing. I met a teacher on a Greyhound Tour and we explored the sights together, even sharing a motel room, as it was a busy season. On my way home, I got the only vacant seat on the train to Chicago. The train was full of a lively group of boys from the East Coast, returning home after a summer at camp. When their counselor finally got them quieted down for the night, the conductor, feeling sorry for me, fixed up a restroom for a sleeping compartment for me. He located three chairs and placed pillows on them before giving me a blanket to put over me. Although it was difficult sleeping, I appreciated his thoughtfulness. At Chicago, I changed to a double-decker Greyhound bus and had a pleasant trip the rest of the way to Binghamton. This was indeed a true ten-day adventure. Tom returned home eleven days later and he and I left the same day for New Jersey to meet Jorette at the Hoboken Pier upon her return from Europe. We drove her back to college four days later.

Tom and Kay were married on November 30, 1957. They had an elaborate wedding in the Catholic Church and large reception at her parent's home. When they returned from a brief wedding trip, they moved in with me for the next fifteen months. Kay had a teaching job while Tom continued his college education. Then they moved to Bloomington, Indiana, where Tom took graduate courses at Indiana University. My first grandchild, Maureen, was born in 1959 while Tom and Kay were in Indiana and I immediately went out to see her. Upon completion of his courses, they returned to live with me until they moved into a trailer several months later.

Jorette graduated from Geneseo State Teachers College in June 1959 and we immediately left for a two-month trip to Europe. Two of Jorette's college classmates accompanied us and my cousin, Caroline Bopp, joined us in London. I arranged for a rental car to meet us at Shannon Airport and we drove over 1,180 miles around Ireland in ten days, then on to Scotland, renting another car and exploring Scotland and England. In London, we met up with a pen pal of Jorette's with whom she had corresponded for seven years. Colin Kitson, a very likeable chap, spent every day with us, guiding us to popular tourist attractions.

We crossed the English Channel on the *Isle of Thanet*. It was a former hospital ship in the Dunkirk Evacuation and saw war service from 1939–1945. After four marvelous days in Paris, we hired another car and drove 3,433 miles through France, Luxemburg, Holland, Germany, Lichtenstein, Austria, and Switzerland. When we reached Vienna, Jorette and I spent several memorable days visiting the Austrian family with whom she had lived two years previously. They treated us like long-lost family members, making a wonderful trip extra-special for us. I planned the entire two-month trip—taking us to many places off the beaten path. We stayed in bed and breakfasts, a nunnery, quaint hotels, small inns, and youth hostels—nothing was fancy but they were all neat and clean. We seldom ate lunch in a restaurant, but preferred to have a snack of cheese and fruit along the roadside. It was an adventure for all of us and we learned to live on $5.00 a day, which was not an easy task. Jorette and the girls did all the driving and the trip was a big success. The total cost of the trip amounted to $950.10.

When we returned home, I immediately went back to work and completed preparations for Jorette's upcoming wedding. She met Lawrence Martin from Carmel, New York, a year earlier and was very much in love. They were married in Greene's Episcopal Church on September 26, 1959, and set up housekeeping in White Plains, New York. Jorette started work as a school librarian and Larry worked for the Traveler's Insurance Company.

In October, I joined the newly formed Historical Society in Greene. The following year I started going to the county clerk's office in Norwich frequently to research old family deeds. I was beginning to collect a lot of information and I worked late into the evening organizing it. In January 1961, the town supervisor, who knew about my interest in history, asked me to accept the new position of town historian.

It was not long before I became a grandmother a second, third, and fourth time. My first grandson, Kevin Martin, was born in 1960, followed by Christopher Cochrane in 1961 and Valerie Martin in 1962—three grandchildren in less than two years. In February 1961, Tom rented their trailer and his family of four came to live with me for the rest of the school year. Tom was teaching at Greene Central School and helping Dick Capra on his dairy farm in the evening. My little house was crowded with five people living in it. I did a lot of babysitting when I was not working at the hospital or reading old *Chenango American* newspapers at the library, and the days just flew by.

In May 1963, I was hanging up curtains in the living room when I slipped off the stool and sprained my ankle. Kay went to the hospital for a pair of crutches so I could get into the doctor's office. Not used to them I fell down the steps on my way to the car. Then on my way into the doctor's office, I lost my balance and fell on the ground hurting my ankle, knee, and left side of my head. Dr. Centerwall helped me in and took X-rays, called the Emergency Squad and sent me to the hospital for five days. In between visitors, I was able to focus upon some historical work that required my attention.

Two months later, Kay drove me to Norwich so I could continue with my research. We stopped beside the road so I could take a picture of a little old hay barn on the river flat south of the city. I slipped on a pebble on an incline and fell. A passerby helped Kay get me into their Volkswagen Microbus and we went directly to the Norwich Hospital where I spent the next eleven days in extreme pain. X-rays showed four fractures in my foot and ankle. The swelling was so great that the doctor could not put a plaster of Paris cast on my foot for ten days, after which time a full leg cast was put on. I do not know how I would have stood it had it not been for a large packet of census statistics for Greene that arrived fortuitously in the mail from the New York State Library. I spent the entire time I was in the hospital copying data to take my mind off the pain. Finally, I was transferred to the Greene Hospital where I was a patient for one month, during which time I could oversee activities, do some office work, and work on historical records. I really enjoyed being a patient and never in my life had so much attention. When it came time to be discharged, I spent the entire morning catching up with every hospital detail I could think of before going home.

I eventually learned to use crutches and got around fairly well. I even went to visit my cousin Catherine in Albany after the removal of the cast in spite of my swollen foot and ankle. I spent two full days at the State Library researching the English family in copious amounts of reference materials. The librarians were just wonderful in bringing books and boxes of records for me to peruse. I never could have done nearly as much, hobbling around on crutches, had they not waited on me. A few days after I returned home, I went back to work, but limited my shift to eight hours a day. That November, my entire family gathered to celebrate Mama's 90th birthday on Thanksgiving Day.

The year 1963 was a year of continuous changes beginning with the birth of Elisabeth Cochrane on January 3. The next month, I went to visit Jorette for a few days, and went into New York City to attend a historians' meeting and did some research at the New York Public Library. During the next few months, there were frequent meetings of the Greene Hospital Association concerning the closing of the hospital. The Catholic Church bought Papa's old farm on Washington Street. Michigan State University accepted Tom to be one of fifteen graduate students to attend a six-week Geology Camp in the Alaskan Ice Fields during the summer. Larry accepted a job at the Raymond Corporation and Jorette and her family moved to Greene. Papa's upstairs apartment was empty, so he suggested that they move in until they needed a larger place. Papa quickly began remodeling the bathroom and installing a bathtub for the children. He was never as happy as when he was remodeling and even happier because Jorette would be living upstairs. After retiring from farming, Papa built fifteen houses and once that got to be too much for him, he kept busy doing all kinds of carpentry, painting, and plumbing for the widows in town. With Jorette living in the house, he would no longer need to worry about Mama being alone when he had a job to do.

Kay and the children lived with me until September and then moved to Bloomington, Indiana, where Tom would finish graduate school. I took time off from work and went along to help Kay set up home in student housing. We were shocked to find the apartment in deplorable condition and had to clean, disinfect, and debug it before unpacking boxes. A few days later, Tom arrived in the Volkswagen Microbus from his trip to Alaska—almost unrecognizable in his beard and whiskers! I left for home on a bus the next day, arriving exhausted twenty-six hours later. It was hard to leave them after they had lived with me for nearly six years, but I was glad to get home and see Jorette and Larry waiting for me at the bus station. Imagine how fortunate I was: one family had moved away and the other had moved to Greene. It seemed I was not destined to be without one of my children nearby, and I was so thankful.

I completely lost my voice on the long bus ride due to the air-conditioning and was unable to return to work for a week, so I started housecleaning, painting, and reorganizing my house. A few weeks later, I bought a new bedroom suite because I had given my set to Tom and Kay, as they needed it. It amused me to think about the number of times I had moved from bedroom to bedroom in the past six years. The first time was when Tom and Kay were married; they moved in with me from December 1957 to February 1959. When they left, I moved back into my room. They returned in June so I moved into Jorette's old room a second time. That summer they bought a trailer when I was in Europe and had it set on the McNulty property, so I again moved back to my room. Then in September 1960, two teachers at GCS boarded with me for the school year and occupied the two single rooms. I lived alone until February 1962 when Tom sold their trailer and they came back to live with me for eighteen months until moving to Indiana.

\* \* \*

Nineteen sixty-three had been such a busy year but one event stands out vividly. One November afternoon, Jorette and her two children and I went for a ride and stopped to see Phyllis Lerwick just as the news came on TV of the assassination of John F. Kennedy. It totally stunned each one of us and shocked the entire nation. Everyone followed the news coverage on television, hungering for the latest detail, until President Kennedy was laid to rest. Next to the bombing of Pearl Harbor, it was the most shocking public event in my lifetime.

I worked my last shift at the Greene Hospital on March 6, 1964, the day the hospital closed. For eighteen years, I had spent a good portion of my life at the hospital and its closing felt like a death in the family to me. I was not old enough to collect Social Security, so I needed to work for two more years. In the following three months, I filled in at the Elizabeth Church Manor Infirmary near Binghamton, the Taylor Nursing Home in Greene and Norwich, and at a doctor's office in Binghamton.

In June, Tom, Kay, and the family came for their last visit before moving to Oklahoma City where Tom had accepted a job with an oil company. Three months later, I flew to Oklahoma City to help take care of their new baby, Brian, born on September 4, 1964. After spending three weeks with them, I went by Greyhound bus to Knoxville, Tennessee, where I took a tour of the Great Smoky Mountains. It was a beautiful trip with the fall colors at their best. During the remainder of the year, I worked twenty-seven (3–11 shifts) at Taylor's Nursing Home and seventeen various shifts at Elizabeth Church Manor. I started taking care of Claribel Cowles on Saturday morning and did so for the next three years.

I was never at a lack of things to do with and for my family in Greene. Early in 1965, Jorette and Larry bought Mrs. Charles Drachler's home on Foundry Street, next door to Papa's, and Mrs. Drachler moved into their apartment. I helped both move. DeeAhn Martin was born on June 2 and I took care of the children while Jorette was in the hospital. My brother's wife, Genevieve, died unexpectedly on July 5— the two of us had attended an ice cream social the previous day! Thereafter, I not only did my parents' laundry but Paul's as well as my own. Paul needed help in sorting through all of Genevieve's belongings and deciding what to keep or to sell. Jorette helped me clean every cupboard and closet and price every item for a sale that went on for ten days.

I was astounded one morning when a Mr. Burrows from Cleveland found me helping Paul with the sale. He was searching for his ancestors. I took him up to my house, spread all of my records on the dining room table and told him to make himself at home. (I trusted everyone!) Then I dashed back down to Paul's house. When I got home at 2:30, Jorette left the baby with me so she could go blackberrying. Then two people knocked on my door looking for information on the Nichols family. In the meantime, Francis Taft was hammering away on the roof, putting new shingles on my house. Mr. Burrows left at 5 p.m. and I cleaned up and dressed to go out for dinner with him at Baron's Inn. After eating, he drove us to Coventry and I showed him where his ancestor had lived. When he left at 9:30, I tried to type but was just too exhausted, so I went to bed. Does anyone have a busier, more hectic, more interesting life than I?

At this same time, Mama was failing fast and I took care of her daily. I spent every morning in August and September helping Paul and then went to care for Mama before going to work at Taylor's from three-to-eleven. During the nine months prior to the closing of the Taylor Nursing Home in Greene on September 19, 1965, I worked there an average of three days a week. When Harry Taylor transferred the patients to his new facility in Norwich, I went with them and I worked there fifty days before finally retiring at the age of sixty-two. I had always loved nursing and caring for people, but after 46 years, I had simply worn out. The Taylor Nursing home paid me $2.00 an hour, the highest hourly pay I had earned.

* * *

Earl Burrows called on me again in November and we copied each other's records before going out to eat. He returned early the next morning and we had breakfast at my house before going to several cemeteries and visiting other town historians. Our last stop was the town clerk's office before having dinner at Baron's Inn. (He eventually published a complete Burrows genealogy and sent a copy to me.)

Two days later, Mama passed away, just nineteen days before her ninety-third birthday. Papa was unable to attend either the calling hours or the funeral and for the next week slept in his chair all the time, not reading or watching TV at all. They had been married sixty-four years and were always devoted to each other. I was very concerned about Papa as he had several blackout spells just before Mama died. However, I was blessed to have him with us another three years before he died.

In January 1966, Tom's family came from Oklahoma for two weeks and after they left, I stayed with Jorette's children for four days when Larry and Jorette went on a business trip to Toronto, Canada. On the way home, a severe snowstorm caused them to be stranded in Batavia for two days because the roads were impassable. The TV weathermen reported this was the worst blizzard in our area in history—snowdrifts were eighteen to twenty feet high. They got home late in the evening and the next day I went up to my house and waded through snow 29 inches deep. It took over an hour to shovel a path from the door to the road. Later that summer, Kay and the children came for a visit when her sister Mary was married in July. It was such a pleasure seeing my grandchildren all together.

Paul sold his house on Washington Street early in 1966 and bought a newer house at 78 North Chenango Street. The property ran down to the river and he was able to keep his boat in the water. He was a happy man being able to go fishing whenever he desired. We were all surprised when Paul announced he was marrying Debby Lorenz in May, less than a year after Genevieve died. They set up housekeeping and were quite suited to one another.

After working for the Raymond Corporation for twenty-five years, Paul retired on January 26, 1967. Paul was hired in 1942 when it was known as the Lyon-Raymond Corporation. At that time the small manufacturing company, located on Foundry Street, manufactured portable stacking trucks to handle the materials other manufacturers were producing and storing for the war. In 1945 there were sixty-five employees and by the end of 1969, employees numbered 850. Paul had wanted to get a job there when came back from California, but they were not hiring during the Depression. However, after the bombing of Pearl Harbor, there was an increased demand for material handling equipment. Paul worked in the machine shop or in the tool room and was able to use some of his electrical engineering skills from the courses he took in California. After retirement, he accepted a job as a part-time security guard for several years. He enjoyed "working at Raymond's," and considered George Raymond Senior a friend.

In March 1968, I took a Trailways bus to Orlando, Florida, to visit a nursing school classmate, an old high school friend, and Elsie and Jim McNulty in Key West. The month-long trip benefited me greatly, as I needed a break. I got home just in time to host an Open House for Papa's ninetieth birthday in early April.

A few days later, Amer Folsom stopped by to chat just as I finished painting my dining room walls. Ever since attending Papa's Open House, Amer had been thinking about both of us being alone and he thought it might be nice to eat out together every now and then. Amer and Bess Folsom had been my neighbors for years. After Bess died, Amer sold his house and moved into an apartment in the old hospital building. I told Amer I was busy for the next six days, but would consider it since he assured me that he had "no ulterior motive." Our first dinner date was dinner at the Oxford Inn, the second, four days later, was at Baron's Inn. Soon he stopped by to see me every day with one excuse or another. We began having lunch at my house and going for rides every evening. When I took care of the children for ten days while Jorette and Larry were in California, Amer took us out for ice cream, mowed my lawn, and did the grocery shopping. We went to Adams, New York, to put geraniums on Amer's family graves and to meet his boyhood friends, to Syracuse to meet his sister, and to Wyckoff, New Jersey, to meet his eldest son.

In less than three months, Amer asked me to marry him. Our families approved, but what would the Catholic

Church say? Although I had been divorced for twenty-one years, I attended Mass faithfully and I did not want to go against the rules of the church; what was I to do?

Therefore, I went to talk to the priest. He could tell I was in a dilemma and his wisdom put me at ease. Father Kelly said, "Mildred, I can't tell you that you can marry Amer, but I am not going to tell you not to marry him." However, should I remarry I could no longer receive the sacraments, such as Communion.

\* \* \*

Amer Folsom and I were married in the Congregational Church on June 24, 1967. We went on a brief four-day honeymoon as I was under the gun to complete the final changes to a book I was writing on the history of Greene. Amer moved in with me and no two people could have been happier. We newlyweds did everything together.

When December came, Amer was as jubilant as I was when we picked up sixteen cartons of *From Raft to Railroad* at Vail-Ballou Press in Binghamton—546 books in all. Now we were in the bookselling business— together.

Our first long trip was to Bedford, Texas, to visit Tom and Kay who had moved there in May. We arrived in time for Christmas and stayed for ten days before driving to New Orleans, Mobile, Alabama, and Lakeland, Florida. We finally arrived home on January 20 after traveling 5,247 miles. In the next few years, Amer and I took several road trips around New York State, Canada, and Nova Scotia, and several trips to Oklahoma City, Omaha, and Wheaton, Illinois, to visit our families.

Amer and I were very happy together. Suddenly, I had a social life that had been nonexistent since World War II. Amer knew everyone in town after being in business in Greene for many years, a member of the Rotary Club, and former council member for the Town of Greene. He was nine years older than I was but age made no difference to us. We belonged to a card club, attended church suppers and dinners at the Grange, and joined the newly formed Senior Citizens Club. We took rides every evening, ate out every Sunday, and always called on Papa after attending church.

Occasionally we helped Elliot out at Folsom's Delicatessen—Amer and Bess were former owners from 1955 to 1963 when Elliot and Janice took it over. They asked us to fill in whenever they were away, and my job was to make large pans of potato and macaroni salad for the store.

*Amer and Mildred Folsom - 1969*

Suddenly there were changes all around us. Amer Jr. moved from New Jersey to Wheaton, Illinois, and Larry resigned from the Raymond Corporation and accepted a position selling forklift trucks in Omaha, Nebraska. Tom's family arrived from Texas for a visit just before he changed jobs and moved his family back to Oklahoma City. After five years, Jorette and her family moved away from Greene. Now both families lived hundreds of miles away and I was so glad that I had Amer to fill the emptiness in my heart. The following spring, Amer and I went to visit all three families.

The day after Christmas in 1969, a record 38 inches of snow fell. Traffic was at a standstill. There were no doctors, drug store, or Emergency Squad available until the next day. I called Papa to see how he was and learned he had a weak spell. I was able to get out of the driveway and catch a ride to town with the fuel oil truck to stay with him. Papa had fallen and said he was in considerable pain. I made him comfortable until the next day, when the Emergency Squad could take him to Lourdes Hospital. The diagnosis was atrial fibrillation, congestion in his right lung, and three broken ribs. In the next five weeks, Papa had his ups and downs, but we got everything ready to bring him home to my house. Then suddenly he was gone, just two months before his ninety-third birthday.

\* \* \*

I inherited Papa's 1849 house on 16 South Chenango Street. Amer and I decided we would rent both apartments, have the house re-wired, and make improvements to the downstairs kitchen and bathroom. We painted everything on the main floor and hired someone to paint the outside of the house. However, after renting the downstairs to two different families, we decided not to rent it again when the second family unexpectedly moved out. Consequently, we put a For Sale sign on both properties and decided to leave it up to the Lord as to which house would be our home. Three months later, we had His answer when we had a buyer for my home on Coventry Road. We sold everything we did not want from my house and moved to the village.

It was sad to leave the house where I had lived for twenty-four happy years.

\* \* \*

*We moved to 16 South Chenango Street in 1971*

Now that we lived in the village, a completely new way of life opened up and I knew it was best for us as we were getting older and I still did not drive. I was surprised how much I liked living downtown. I could walk to the grocery store, the library, or town offices in a matter of minutes. Once again, I was involved in planting new flowerbeds around the foundation of the house and a profusion of blooms rewarded my efforts. We planted morning glories along the back porch and trained them to climb 10 feet high on cords. Amer attached flower boxes to the wrap-around front porch railing on the east and south side of the house. The house and small corner lot never looked so beautiful.

We had so much more freedom without the large lawn to mow and flowerbeds to weed. Now I had time to engage in more volunteer work and participate in activities that had been out of the question before. I was invited to join the Philomath Club, a group of women who met monthly to discuss "good reading." For many years, I enjoyed the fellowship of those women whose interests were similar to my own. Everything about this change in my life was so positive, but then came a change I did not foresee—Tom and Kay were separating! I was overwhelmed with sadness.

Tom brought his girlfriend to visit us in November and again in June 1973. I continued to be in close contact with Kay as she was like a daughter to me. Amer was not up to a long trip that year, so I went to Omaha alone by Greyhound to visit the Martins for Christmas, then by bus to visit Tom and Ann, as well as Kay and the children. In July, my friend Tyl and I attended the fiftieth anniversary of our class at the Albany Hospital. I had had a head cold for two weeks and could barely speak aloud at the reunion but tried so hard that my voice was completely gone for over a week. Jorette and the children visited us for three weeks later that summer and Larry joined them for one week. Everyone liked the changes that Amer and I had made to Papa's house.

In January, Amer was not feeling well and went to see Dr. Centerwall, who immediately called the Emergency Squad to take him to Lourdes Hospital. He was in and out of the hospital for three months, before passing away. Amer died on April 23, 1975, and I became a widow after eight wonderful years together. Within a day or so, Jorette and Tom arrived for Amer's funeral. Tom bought Amer's car and drove home to Oklahoma City. Although I was very lonesome those first few weeks, I immediately went back to helping at 60-Plus, working at the blood bank and at a hearing clinic, and giving flu shots to the senior citizens. I knew I had to keep busy and not wallow in my grief. Like all of life's sorrows, it took time to adjust to being alone once again but I managed with the help of Paul and Debby and other friends. In July, my ten-year-old granddaughter DeeAhn Martin came to visit me for a month and we had a wonderful time together. She lifted my spirits and was just the right tonic to cure my melancholy. On August 13, I traveled with her to Omaha and then headed south to visit the two families in Oklahoma City.

Three months after DeeAhn's visit, I was surprised to receive a phone call from Ed Hutchinson saying that he needed a sales manager for Page Print and wondered if Larry would be interested. Larry flew out a few days after speaking to Ed and accepted the job. He stayed with me, started house hunting and eventually bought a 100-year-old house at 60 North Chenango Street. We both agreed it would be perfect for the family. Jorette and the children left Omaha after school ended and arrived in Greene two days before Christmas. They lived at my house until their furniture arrived in January. I was delighted to have Jorette and Larry and their children return to Greene. I had been alone for eight months—now the Lord had brought my daughter and her family home. Oh, how blessed I am!

* * *

While the Martins were settling into their home, I was involved in numerous activities whose focus was the bicentennial anniversary of our nation. Due to the popularity of quilts, I conceived the idea of organizing a community quilting project. Since quilting was a creative outlet for women, possibly dating back to the time of the Revolution, it seemed that raffling off a quilt would be an appropriate fund-raiser to support our local bicentennial celebration the following year. I made my own patterns for a traditional *log cabin* quilt and more than twenty-five women participated in the project. Many other residents donated materials for it.

Others heard of the project and more than twenty women volunteered to make craft items for the Senior Citizens' booth at the bicentennial celebration—the proceeds also going to defray the expenses of the celebration. We held fifteen work meetings at my home. Many planning meetings and all the quilting sessions took place at my house as well. My home had never seen such activity. Ladies were in and out at all hours of the day, making blocks for the log cabin quilt, sewing them together, and eventually hand quilting the nearly finished product. I loved the sense of unity we developed as we worked together to make "something" lovely out of all those pieces of material. Quilts had been a part of my growing up, but I had never made one nor had I organized any community project of this scope. I felt very fond of my co-workers and hated to see the project end. I also learned that I enjoyed quilting and made four quilts in the years that followed.

For the next eight years, my life not only revolved around my activities but around the Martin family as well. Paul, Debby, and I spent the major holidays with Jorette's family and we enjoyed watching her three children grow up. Now, it was my turn to help Jorette can and freeze vegetables from their huge garden. Paul was teaching Kevin to fish and hunt. I enjoyed the children stopping at my house on their way home from school and getting to know five Rotary exchange students who lived at their house during the time Valerie and DeeAhn were in high school. When Jorette accepted a job managing the Canal Mall Bake Shop, I gave her an extra hand during the opening day celebration. She encouraged me to join the Garden Club and I enjoyed their interesting meetings, working at the flower shows and weeding the tree wells along Genesee Street until I was in my eighties.

I looked forward to my grandchildren's visits and always had sugar cookies on hand to share with them. In nice weather, we would sit on the porch and talk about all the exciting things that were happening in their lives. When the children learned to drive, each one was happy to drive me wherever I needed to go. Kevin mowed my small lawn and shoveled the snow off the sidewalks. After he left for college, DeeAhn took over the mowing. Jorette invited me to every graduation party and going-away parties for exchange students and I was always eager to help her in any way I could. She hosted a family reunion on Paul's seventy-fifth birthday by inviting our first cousins on the English side of the family to an outdoor picnic. We had not gotten together for years and so it was a real treat for all of us.

Some people slow down when they are in their seventies, but that was not true in my case. I volunteered at 60-Plus luncheons three times a week, and attended monthly meetings of the Philomath Club and the Garden Club; I worked at the Church Bazaar and Greene Garden Club Flower Shows, at every blood bank and at the Food Tent on Labor Day. I went on bus trips with the senior citizens group and enjoyed life to the fullest. My grandchildren often said, "Grandma, you are the busiest woman in town."

*Mildred and her grandchildren — Valerie, DeeAhn, and Kevin Martin*

Three years after Jorette and her family moved back to Greene, my grandson Kevin graduated from Greene High School. He received a $1,050 award from the Raymond Corporation and entered Clarkson University in the fall. Valerie graduated two years later in 1980. She received a four-year state scholarship and after going to France as a Rotary Exchange Student, she attended Binghamton University. The years were going by too fast—DeeAhn went through high school in three years and left for Cape Town, South Africa, as the second Rotary Exchange Student in our family. Upon her return, DeeAhn entered Lycoming College in Williamsport, Pennsylvania. I believe my love of learning and love of traveling rubbed off on some of my grandchildren.

I missed the frequent interaction with my grandchildren once they graduated from high school. I knew that Jorette would want to go back to work and, sure enough, shortly after DeeAhn left home, the Binghamton Press hired Jorette to be its library director. Both Larry and Kevin worked for companies in Binghamton and Valerie lived at college, so I no longer saw the family as often. My new role was taking care of Patches, the family beagle. Jorette dropped the dog off on her way to work and picked her up at the end of the day. It did not surprise me when they began to talk about moving closer to work.

The following March, Jorette and Larry bought a town-house in Binghamton and Kevin moved into an apartment not far from them. I helped them pack boxes. On moving day, I rode to Binghamton with Peg Marr who transported the tall antique mirror that once belonged to my parents to their new home.

I was glad to have so many genealogy requests and other projects to keep me busy after Jorette and Larry moved to Binghamton. People were always in and out of my house for genealogy information, to pick up Senior Citizen Discount cards, or just to chat. It was not my nature to sit idle, so I always had a needlework project in progress. One of my challenges was making a crazy quilt out of neckties.

\* \* \*

One evening I sat down to watch television. I happened to turn to the World Literature Crusade, curious to see what it was all about, when the host of the program asked viewers to pray fifteen minutes a day for unsaved people in the world. He wanted listeners to participate in a 24-hour prayer-chain and encouraged us to tell them when we would be willing to pray. The program was nearly over when I found myself at my phone dialing that number. From that moment on, I was a different person. Fifteen minutes praying for others became thirty and thirty minutes became an hour. I read my Bible and every Christian publication I could get my hands on. I started watching Christian evangelists on TV and supporting several ministries. The more I gave the more came back to me. I began to attend Bible studies at the Methodist Church and was surprised at how little I knew about the Bible. My relationship with the Lord grew stronger once I put my faith in Jesus Christ rather than in church membership. In my heart, I knew that faith in Christ and nothing else was the key to salvation.

Christian programs on television became part of my daily routine and the messages I heard had an incredible impact upon my thinking. Many of my beliefs were no longer consistent with those I had learned as a child. I had not been taught that Christianity is primarily a relationship with Jesus Christ, rather than adherence to the rules and rituals set down by one denomination or another. However, when it came to worshipping God, I had a reverence for the liturgy of the Catholic Church and continued to find the Mass relevant and meaningful.

I welcomed the efforts of the Catholic Charismatic Renewal movement to renew the life of the Church. In 1984, the U. S. Bishops recognized that renewal was positive and had brought personal spiritual renewal to the lives of millions of Catholics deepening their love for Jesus Christ, the Holy Spirit, and Scripture. When Father Dietrich announced a six-week course to discuss renewal, I was eager to attend. I was so encouraged that I took along my "Renewal Suggestions" — nine pages of my thoughts—which the group asked me to read. Everyone liked the points I made and most were surprised at the many Bible passages that I included. All wanted copies and decided to use it for the theme.

Renew groups stated meeting at individual homes after the six-week class ended. I joined a Bible Study/Prayer group that met bi-weekly at Ray and Midge Stanton's home. Our group spearheaded a used-clothing drive to send clothes to a relief agency in Appalachia. We sorted many bags of clothing in my garage and ended up sending 22 cartons of clothing to Kentucky the day before Thanksgiving. Our renew group continued to meet for eighteen months. Once it disbanded, I missed the fellowship and studying the Bible together.

In May 1984, Jorette and I flew from Binghamton to San Francisco where Tom and Ann met us. The next morning, we drove north along the Pacific coast on Route 1 for about 100 miles until we reached the Sea Ranch. Tom had built a large home overlooking the ocean and we were very impressed by all he had done. We enjoyed daily walks along the bluffs, through redwood forests and short trips to the charming coastal village of Gualala, about four miles north of Sea Ranch. What makes the Sea Ranch so unique is its distinctive architecture. The buildings, designed to blend into their surroundings, are clad in wooden siding or shingles with no paint to draw attraction to the buildings. It was unlike any other place I had ever visited.

\* \* \*

Later that summer, I attended a meeting at the Village Office concerning a possible residence for Senior Citizens. The main objection for the Birdsall Street location concerned the "swampy zone" under consideration. I believed Greene needed senior citizen housing, and might consider living there if it materialized. Twenty months later the obstacles were resolved and construction began.

In the fall of 1984, the Philomath Club promoted a Used Book Sale at the Moore Memorial Library. It was a tremendous amount of work for our small club and we appreciated others who pitched in to help us. We spent untold hours in the basement sorting "tons" of old books and magazines—an arduous task for women of our age. I put in seventy-two hours sorting books, setting up and working at the three-day sale. Consequently, our efforts were rewarded by netting $700 that Philomath presented to the Library Board.

\* \* \*

Residents in Greene can never say there is nothing to do. Each July, the Greene Chamber of Commerce sponsors an Arts and Crafts Fair in Greene's downtown district. This event started in 1976, and by 1985 had become a popular festival. That year I volunteered to work at the Revitalization Exhibit booth near the library from 9 to 11 and 12:30 to 3:00. Our booth sold balloons for fifty cents each. It had been a lovely 80-degree day and I stood up most of the time. I left just after 3 p.m. and walked up West Genesee St. to view the museum's displays of early history. When I stopped to visit with friends, I suddenly got so dizzy that a friend had to walk me home. I nearly passed out when I got in the house. After a cold drink, and once I had sufficiently recovered, she left. I spent the remainder of the evening on the couch. I wondered if this was a warning for me to slow down, hoping my dizziness was only due to being out in the heat all day.

The biggest event of the year in Greene is the annual Labor Day Picnic. This community-wide event began in 1919 as a celebration of the harvest. My parents always looked forward into seeing old friends and playing bingo in the Bingo Tent, while I looked forward to volunteering at the Council of Churches Food Tent. The success of our community celebration was due to the many residents who volunteer in different capacities year after year. Labor Day events always begin with hose fights on Genesee Street, followed by a parade to the Ball Flats where there are amusement rides, food booths, and family attractions and activities throughout the day, ending with a fireworks finale. It is a tradition for many local residents to walk around the athletic field (or grounds) looking to meet relatives and acquaintances among the crowd as well as working at the various concessions.

For a number of years, I volunteered to help make baked beans and salad dressing, or prepare the chicken barbeque sauce. The volunteer firemen are experts at grilling several thousand chicken halves and everyone says we serve the best chicken BBQ of any town in the area. Women in the community make homemade pies and cupcakes and no matter how many pies we have, they are gone long before the last chicken is sold. Volunteers from all the churches staff the Food Tent and everyone is so friendly and amiable. The profit from the Food Tent supports scholarships, the Summer Recreation Program, Community Youth Services and the Greene Emergency Squad.

I worked at the Food Tent and then at the Revitalization display in the Scout house for the last time in 1985. After standing for most of the afternoon, I had a dizzy spell and had to sit down. I hated to admit that I was getting older but I knew my days of volunteering were coming to an end.

Then in December, failing health prompted me to think about selling my house. When I was shoveling the sidewalk early one winter morning, I tore a muscle in my chest without realizing it. Within a few days, I developed an erratic heartbeat and I started to tire easily and have no energy. Dr.

Centerwall sent me to see a cardiologist but the medicine he prescribed made me feel worse. After six months of not feeling up to par, I doubted the doctors would find the reason I felt so poorly. Realizing the house was just too much for me, Mrs. Palmiter, my upstairs tenant, and I started talking about moving into the new Senior Citizens' Residence. Jorette and Larry were supportive of my decision, and by the summer of 1986, I placed my house in the hands of a real estate broker.

# Chapter 13

---

# My Work as Town Historian

---

*Do not go where the path may lead,*
*Go instead where there is no path and leave a trail.*
—Ralph Waldo Emerson

In November of 1960, the Town Board of Greene appointed me the first historian for the Town of Greene. At that time, the state of New York wanted all towns to have a local historian. Since I was engaged in collecting information and photographs about portions of the history of the town and village of Greene, Paul English, the town supervisor, asked me to accept that position. A small grant went with the appointment. It allowed me to carry on research and have access to certain records about the early settlers and their activities. When I accepted the post, the duties of a town historian were not well defined. In the first year, I blocked out several important areas: keeping records of existing cemeteries and who was buried in them; obtaining old deeds and old maps of the area; and making history come alive for the younger members of the community.

I never imagined that my interest in family genealogy would lead to becoming a town historian! I had always been interested in history and enjoyed reading about the history of places I wanted to visit before setting off on my travels. With Tom and Jorette away at college, I realized I had time to devote to my own interests. My first goal was to delve into the English and Justen family genealogies.

When I was a young girl, my family often visited old family friends or relatives on Sunday afternoons. I would listen to my father's family talk about the past and it sparked my interest in my family's background. Rather than being bored, I found it fascinating to listen to their stories and look though old books and assorted memorabilia. Never did I dream that years later my interest in the history of the English family would lead to a fervid interest in the early history of Greene.

My father was knowledgeable about his family's background. His great-grandfather, Nathaniel English, came to Greene from Connecticut in 1815. Papa remembered a lot about other family members and knew the burial sites of many of his father and grandfather's generation. The first thing we did was to visit local burial grounds and cemeteries to locate family gravesites so I could record their names and vital statistics. Papa drove us to all the cemeteries within the town of Greene— every single one of them. Not only did I copy down the information of our family members, but also I copied down the names and dates listed on every gravestone in the cemetery! Most of those small graveyards were in a deplorable state—completely overgrown with briars, with broken fences and gravestones that were becoming illegible due to weathering. I was afraid that within another one or two generations, the information would be lost. It was not long before I became interested in other families as I located headstones belonging to the Ketchum, Juliand, Gray, Harrington, Birdsall, and Race families to name but a few of the early inhabitants of Greene. I am so glad I took time to copy every headstone we found because the information proved invaluable over the years.

My interest in the Greene area also sprang from investigating the history of our former residences on the Van Valkenburgh and Juliand farms. Visits to county courthouses to search deed and family records and reading old Chenango Americans led me to discover how little was easily accessible on the history of Greene. Local histories about other communities in Chenango County existed but not about the major events and changes in the Town of Greene from its origin to the present day. Therefore, I determined to find out as much as I could about my hometown.

One of my greatest pleasures in digging into the past was talking to elderly residents whose reminiscences of past events and tales of family history were priceless. My work in the Greene Hospital opened the doors to many conversations about the "old days in Greene." Knowing of my interest, many people invited me to their homes to look at old account books, diaries, journals and letters that had been handed down from generation to generation. I often felt like I had stepped back in time.

I never intended to be deeply involved with genealogical research, but so many people wrote to me about their ancestry that my interest intensified as I helped others with their family research. In my second year as historian, I answered letters from people all over the county who were tracing their family tree and needed information on ancestors who had lived in Greene. I could just go to my cemetery records and there it was. I kept a record of the information I unearthed so it would be readily available to others. I joined the newly formed Central New York Genealogical Society to learn new ideas and tips to help ancestor hunters locate information about family members who once lived in this area. Genealogists from around the country showed up on my doorstep, some spending hours with me, others several days, and I corresponded with a handful for a few years.

In 1963, I started receiving a stipend of $100 a year from the Town of Greene for my services as town historian. I became interested in local censuses and copied the 1850 and 1855 census for the Town of Greene from Norwich records. I reported to the state, "Found it necessary to card index these censuses, which proved to be my big project for the year." The earlier censuses from 1800, 1810, 1820, and 1840 were not available locally, so I wrote to the State Department in Albany and they made copies to send to me. I added all the names to my index cards, and before long there were nearly 3,000 cards in my file taking in the years 1800, 1810, 1820, 1830, 1850, and 1855—and these were only for the Town of Greene. I wanted to do the same for Coventry and Smithville in as much as they tied in so closely with Greene, so I began to trade material with other historians to save us all time and money. What would have been a tedious task for someone else was interesting for me because I enjoyed copying censuses and discovering family relationships.

After five years of collecting information about the early history of Greene, I was convinced others would be interested in what I was discovering, but I was hesitant to produce a book of my research. I never intended to write a book, let alone two books—everything I put down on paper was going to be an article about a particular topic, such as Greene's early history, its settlers, schools, businesses, or landmarks. Every day I found more information, so I wrote and rewrote and re-rewrote again until I realized I had accumulated so much information that it would be a shame not to publish it. Other town historians, local officials, and acquaintances encouraged me to go forward with publishing a history of Greene, so I eventually did.

In December 1966, I included the following in my yearly town historian's report to the town supervisor,

> *The first six months of 1966 included the usual duties of the historian, more research, copying records, and reading six years of old Chenango American files. In July, I stopped working entirely for five months in order to devote full time to getting the history of Greene written and published by Greene's 175$^{th}$ anniversary in 1967.*

My first book, *From Raft to Railroad,* was published 175 years from the time of the first settlement in Greene and on the 125$^{th}$ anniversary of the incorporation of the village. This comprehensive history of early settlers and their activities covered the years from 1792 to 1867. The book includes maps, photographs, censuses from 1800 through 1855, and translation of French letters. The information came from a variety of sources including old books, diaries, letters, newspapers, censuses, deeds, family records in Bibles, and other sources. I believe my book's usefulness for future researchers would be to include an index, the outgrowth of my extensive card file of the early settlers in Greene. The thirty-two-page index took hours to cross-check, but all my life I had followed Henry Wadsworth Longfellow's principle of "*doing what you can do well, and doing well whatever you do,*" thus I could not do otherwise. After the manuscript was in the hands of Cayuga Press, I breathed a sigh of relief and turned my attention to my new husband, Amer Folsom, whom I had married in June. I knew that once the book was released at the end of the year, I would be busier than ever.

When *Raft to Railroad* was finally published, many local residents asked me when a sequel would be forthcoming. Therefore, I began to formulate my ideas for a second book although I found it easier to focus on smaller projects for the next year or so. Then I got serious about finishing my research. Due to the popularity of my first book, more sources of information became available to me when the word got around that I was investigating the history and interesting events that had occurred in Greene from 1867 to 1967. Older residents stepped forward to share their memories with me. Many of their historical anecdotes verified stories from old newspapers and often revealed new tidbits of information. When I needed to delve into the history of present-day businesses and industries, Amer drove me to wherever I needed to go to gather information for the second book.

Little by little, all the information I had took shape. I filed and documented everything, which until now were just scattered threads of history. When I presented my yearly report in 1969, I reported:

*Finished making a card index file of deaths taken from the Town Clerk's records and newspaper obituaries—cemetery records are now being added. Finished a survey of Greene's former rural school districts for the Chenango County files—this turned into a 92-page report including several pages of pictures. I made a duplicate copy to keep here in Greene...Each local historian is now requested to make a similar survey of the churches in her town. This should be a simple project for me as I have already researched the history and acquired pictures of all the churches in Greene.*

In 1971, I completed the sequel to my first book, titling it *Echoes of the Past—Annals of the Town of Greene—1867–1967*. Newspaper articles such as the following one in the *Norwich Evening Sun* resulted in an immediate demand for my second book.

> If Mrs. Folsom has left anything historically important out of Echoes of the Past, about Greene's history, it is not apparent. Her undertaking is much like an information almanac. It provides vivid and interesting descriptions and narratives of highlights in her town's history on one hand, and on the other comes up with names and statistics so useful to the historian, writer and researcher who may later want to develop some aspect of Greene's history.
>
> Her jammed-packed book even includes pertinent assessment rolls, the roll of various cemeteries and other statistics, which the genealogists, in particular, will find invaluable. But the non-Greene resident—and perhaps the Greene resident, too—will find the history of the town's colorful past most interesting.[9]

The exposure from the media was what I needed to promote sales of both books. The demand for the more recent history was immediate and people continuously appeared on my doorstep to purchase one or more copies. I enjoyed writing the two books so much, that I never considered making a profit from either of them, so I sold them at cost. My one desire was to put this information into the hands of others who have a deep interest in Greene and its heritage. I also hoped that present and future generations of Greene residents would find the history of our small community as fascinating as I did and would take pride in their heritage.

\* \* \*

Early in 1975, I became a widow. Once again, I chose to assess my life and decide what goals I wanted to achieve as town historian. As I considered several projects to pursue,

---

[9] Joe Quinn, "Book Colorfully Records Century of Greene's Past," *Evening Sun*, Nov. 26, 1971, p. 3

my mind focused upon ways our community could observe the bicentennial celebration of our country. By the end of the year, our plans were well under way. In 1976, I attended ten Bicentennial Committee meetings, many held at my house. I attended one museum meeting at the Moore Memorial Library, one meeting of town historians in Norwich, and made nine trips to the county clerk's office. Someone suggested it would be nice to encourage owners of the oldest homes in the village to display a plaque identifying the year of construction. I was one of the first residents to do so. I was proud to display "1849" on my house on 16 South Chenango Street as well as helping other homeowners confirm the year their house was built.

My next project was writing several local history articles for the *Chenango American* and a short contrasting history of Greene—then and now—for a souvenir newspaper, *The Bicentennial Times*. It contained five self-guided tours of the village that I thought people would find interesting. Then I composed twenty-five *Bicentennial Minute* anecdotes for the 60-Plus Dinner Club. Next, I was asked to date and caption 100 slides of old pictures of Greene and vicinity and to narrate the slide presentation. I also volunteered to type the three-act play, written and produced for our two-day celebration on Flag Day weekend. Nearly a thousand people attended the bicentennial play at the high school auditorium on the two nights it was presented. My daughter Jorette, her son Kevin, and I (three generations of my family) had parts in the play. Kevin had the part of Phil in "Canal Canoodling" and Jorette and I appeared in the Civil War scenes. There was a two-hour parade on Saturday and more than 1,200 visitors to the museum. Everyone worked together admirably to make Greene's celebration of the United States Bicentennial a huge success.

The following October, I was utterly surprised when the Business and Professional Women's Club honored me as Woman of the Year for the service I rendered to the community over the years and during the bicentennial. I did not know how to react, as I never sought public recognition and felt embarrassed by all the attention. I always considered it a privilege to have a part in serving my community but the pleasure derived from congratulations from family and good friends far outweighed the surprise and self-consciousness it caused me.

* * *

I think it is important for future generations to understand the historic preservation movement in our country during the second half of the twentieth century. The National Historic Preservation Act of 1966 aimed to promote the preservation, enhancement, and productive use of the historic resources in our country. It established the *National Register of Historic Places* as the official list of the nation's historic places worthy of preservation. The new Act redefined the concept of historic districts and recognized that in many instances it is necessary to not only preserve a building, but also the historic context in which it and other adjacent buildings are placed. Therefore, the idea of designating groupings of buildings caused a significant shift in the concept of historic designations.

State initiatives followed in the next few years due to two major concerns. The number one concern resulted from the large number of historic structures and landmarks that were vanishing without any regard of their value or any consideration of preserving them. The second concern pertained to a belief that structures with a special architectural, historic, or cultural significance enhance the quality of life.

In the 1970s, an interest in historic preservation became popular nationwide due to urban renewal and the building of new highways. Preservationists found themselves in continuous battle with development. It was not long before some citizens in Greene realized that our community would not be immune from the pace of change that threatened to obscure the visible reminder of Greene's historic past. They believed the option open to us to preserve our historic downtown was to protect its unique business district by seeking a landmark status.

William House, Amy Marsland, and I spearheaded a group of citizens to form what became known as the Greene Historical Preservation group. Along with local municipal officials, about twenty of us worked diligently to educate the public on the value of historic preservation. The *Chenango American*, our local newspaper, and all civic groups backed our efforts 100 percent. A majority of citizens believed the business district and park on Genesee Street deserved recognition status as many of the buildings dated to the early 1800s.

In January 1975, William House, Chairman of Greene Historical Preservation, submitted thirty-two building inventory forms for commercial enterprises in the main business district of Greene to the NYS Division of Historic Preservation. I worked with Bill to update any information that I might have omitted in *From Raft to Railroad* and helped research the history of every building and house within the proposed Greene Historic District. Amy Marsland photographed all the buildings under consideration.

When I began to search public records of deed transfers, I became totally absorbed with gathering the history and ownership of every property within the village. The exchange of property down through the years fascinated me. As I conducted my research, many family names appeared repeatedly. Soon, they became as familiar to me as the people I meet on the street.

In 1977, I began probing into the history of every house within the incorporated village of Greene. This project was a result of the historic preservation initiative encouraged by New York State Parks and Recreation Division of Historic Preservation. Each house needed to be identified according to street location, ownership, and type of building material and structural system. In addition, other information concerning outbuildings, surroundings, and notable features had to be recorded.

Norma Davis volunteered to assist me in collecting the information and photographing each house. It was enjoyable working together on a project of this size and it would have taken much longer had I done it by myself. Neither of us drove, so we walked up and down every street in the village, taking photographs, jotting down notes, and verifying every essential piece of information. Then I was ready to identify the date of original construction and builder of each house as well as the history of ownership and date of transfer of each piece of property down through the years. To do that, it was necessary to consult the public records of deed transfers at the Chenango County Clerk's Office, thus requiring many trips on the mini-bus to Norwich to copy down all available information.

It took nine months to document the history of the entire 545 houses in Greene—from July 1977 to March 1978. Completing the building-structure form for each house also took considerable time. Many evenings I worked late into the night typing, attaching a photograph and map showing the location of each property in relation to streets, intersections or other widely recognized features to the form. When the project was complete, I made five copies of each form and assembled them in black binders, so the information would be accessible for generations to come.

In the meantime, we waited patiently to learn the status of our application for historical recognition. The Rosekrans Building in the Village of Greene was the first building to be listed as an historic structure in 1979. The Greene Historical Preservation group worked hard to achieve that designation and it provided the stimulus we needed to request the business district be nominated to the *National Register of Historic Places*.

Many of Greene's leading citizens recognized the benefits of establishing the Greene Historic District. We responded to many deadlines with one report after another. In January 1982, more than thirty area residents including several village officials met with Larry Gobrecht, Coordinator of the National Register Survey Unit, to discuss the benefits of being listed in the State and National Registers of Historic Places. He explained that

> Registered properties will receive a measure of protection from the effect of federal and state agency sponsored or assisted projects. At the same time, a property owner can do whatever he wants to do with his property, whereas the area is protected from state and federal government only. Federal Income Tax credits benefit the owners in certified rehabilitation of the property. Another benefit is that federal and state

agencies are required by law to seek listed historic buildings for leasing. [10]

The proposed Historic District included 11 Birdsall Street, all properties between Jackson Street and Genesee Street, Canal Street, the east and west sides of Chenango Street from 40 North Chenango to 43 South Chenango Street, all properties from 4 East Genesee Street to 73 West Genesee and all properties on Jackson Street.[11] For nearly eight years, we worked hard to achieve our goal and we had won the backing of businesses and property owners and sponsorship of the Raymond Corporation.

In October 1982, the New York State Historic Preservation Office notified the Village of Greene that the proposed historic district in the Village of Greene was approved and listed on the *National Register of Historic Places,* making it the eighth area in Chenango County to achieve national listing. At last, our efforts to protect our community's historical resources had come to fruition. Those of us who had worked diligently to achieve recognition were overjoyed! The Greene Historic District was added to the National Register on September 9, 1982. Its reference number is 82003350. Included are 141 buildings located on 580 acres in the center of the village.[12]

It seemed that each year, changes were occurring in Greene and I was called on for historical information on one place or another. Ten days before the Open House at the restored Sherwood Hotel on January 28, 1979, I recorded a talk about the Sherwood Hotel to air on the radio. I thoroughly researched the history of the Sherwood and was very pleased with the historical brochure that Ed and Sally McGowan had printed for the occasion. Most residents did not know that the stately hotel originally opened on May 1, 1913. I was nine years old at the time and I have many fond

---

[10] "Preservation Official Explains Listing Benefits," *Chenango American*, January 13, 1982, p. 1

[11] For additional information, go to www.livingplaces.com/NY/Chenango_County/Greene_Village/Greene_Historic_District.html

[12] www.nps.gov/nr.research

memories of events that I attended there over the years. The Sherwood operated under various ownerships until 1959, when a new owner decided to refurbish it. Just before it opened for business, a fire broke out on October 20, 1962, causing so much damage that the building was boarded up and left standing as is for seventeen years. Almost two decades later, Ed and Sally McGowan had a dream to restore the hotel to its former elegance and to the delight of the community, it reopened in January 1979. Two months later, on March 19, the new town office building was dedicated. I was a guest of the Town Board at a brunch held at the Sherwood. After the invocation, I was the first speaker to be introduced and I read my history of the town offices.

In 1983, the Town Board raised my historian's salary to $500. On June 16, I went to a dinner at the Norwich Country Club with Mayor Roy Fyfe for a presentation of Historic Preservation Awards.

Looking back over twenty-five years, I know that being town historian brought many new challenges into my life and made life interesting. It might be a college student coming to interview me, or it could be a lawyer from White Plains seeking to verify living relatives in order to settle an estate. I met so many interesting people—professors, lawyers, an Episcopalian bishop from New York, a housewife from Idaho, and untold ancestor hunters. Many people helped me to know the families of our early settlers better because many researchers eagerly gave me as much information as I gave them.

When I first became interested in Greene's history, I found that research was extremely time consuming because the sources of information were all in different locations. I delved into caches in Norwich, Albany, Binghamton, and the local library, town and village offices, cemeteries and into the personal possessions of local residents. People were just wonderful, going all out to help me. They opened attics and cellars—and I pawed through numerous old trunks and boxes. It has been a lot of fun, but all good things must come to an end.

On January 20, 1987, I resigned as the Town of Greene historian. After twenty-five years, I felt it was time for me to step down and turn my records over to a younger person. This decision coincided with my decision to sell my home on South Chenango Street and move into the new senior citizens housing complex on Birdsall Street. Once I moved, I would no longer have space to store all my records and to be honest, I believed the job was too much for an eighty-two year old woman. I continued to help my successor, Barbara Vanderbunt, whenever I could point her in the right direction to locate a specific piece of information. When Barbara found the demands of the historian's work too time consuming in addition to her job, Millie Pixley was appointed town historian in 1988. In an article in the *Chenango American*, Millie Pixley was quoted as saying, "It is Mildred Folsom who has broken the ground for the history of this area: those who come after must forever build on her foundation."

By 1990, a new generation was interested in the history of Greene. Many people wanted to get their hands on my books. Several people asked me to reprint them, but I felt it was a task beyond my capabilities. Jorette was so involved in her job at New York State Electric & Gas that she could not take on the project. Therefore, we decided that it would be best to give permission to the Greene Historical Society to reprint both books so they would remain in circulation and be available to future generations. During the Greene Chamber of Commerce Craft Fair in July 1991, the reprinted books were for sale outside a bookstore on Genesee Street. Millie Pixley asked me to be present to autograph the reprints as well as any first editions that people wanted autographed. I was surprised that after two or three hours, I had signed eighty-seven books and talked to many more people who just stopped to say hello.

Then, on March 14, 1992, the Greater Greene Chamber of Commerce honored me as Citizen of the Year at the Chamber's annual dinner at the Silo Restaurant.

*Receiving award as Citizen of the Year from Millie Pixley*

*Mildred with Larry and Jorette Martin, Tom
Cochrane, and Fran and Dick Capra (cousin)*

I was so happy that Tom, Jorette, and Larry were with me as I would have been overwhelmed had they not been by my side. It was a very happy occasion for me and my family.

The following week, the *Chenango American* reported:

> Millie Pixley, current historian, presented a capsule view of the life and career of Mildred Folsom, Greene's Citizen of the Year. Her long nursing career led to Mildred being Superintendent of the Greene Hospital. When she became town historian, she had no idea what a town historian was supposed to do, but she read years and years' worth of Chenango Americans, town records and individual diaries and has provided the community with an extensive and accurate picture of our community.
>
> Her mastery of our history was invaluable in the writing of her two published books "From Raft to Railroad" and "Echoes of the Past". The books were reprinted by the Greene Chamber in conjunction with our Bicentennial and made available in July '91. About half of the 500 copies have already sold . . . All of her material has proved invaluable in planning for Greene's Bicentennial celebration.
>
> As our Citizen of the Year, Mildred Folsom received much deserved recognition which she very modestly accepted. There was a plaque from the Chamber and a special cross-stitch lovingly done and framed from the Chamber. In addition, she received proclamations from the Town of Greene, from Assemblyman "Rapp" Rappleyea and Senator Tom Libous.[13]

In the quarter of a century that I served my community as town historian, I collected memorabilia of the past such as old scrapbooks, photographs, Greene Fair programs, deeds, account books, and maps. I stored these at my house until I turned all my collections and indexes and other materials over to the town upon my retirement.

My work as town historian was always a labor of love. I uncovered new interests and new ways of helping others, which had been my destiny from the beginning. I am the last

---

[13] "Greater Greene Chamber Meets, Recognizes its Citizen of the Year," *Chenango American*, March 17, 1992, p. 1

of six generations to make Greene my permanent home. I hope that my offspring will visit my hometown someday and when they do, see it through my eyes. No matter how far I have traveled from Greene, the path always led me back home, back home to Greene.

# Chapter 14

## Homeward Bound

*Let me but live my life from year to year,*
*With forward face and unreluctant soul.*
*I shall grow old, but never lose life's zest,*
*Because the road's last turn will be the best.*
—Henry Van Dyke

I have never enjoyed books that leave the reader wondering how the story ended. I often heard genealogists remark, "I wish I could find more information about my great-grandfather" or "I wonder what happened to the family after they moved away." Individuals may think that their life is uninteresting, but perhaps it will be invaluable to someone who reads it in a future generation. How does anyone write a historical novel if stories of ordinary people do not exist to give them an idea for a plot? Keeping a diary affirms the reality of your life and in my case has been useful in compiling my memoirs.

The stories that I remember seem like they took place only yesterday. Time moves so quickly. As I think about the past, I see how clearly Greene is the thread that holds each piece of my life together. When I go for walks around the village in the evening, I envision some of the places as they looked when I was young. I cannot walk north on Canal Street without visualizing the Greene High School that I attended. It was torn down in 1959. When I walk by the former hospital, I remember people and events that were a part of my life. The dilapidated Catholic Church has become an eyesore, but it reminds me of taking Tom and Jorette to their first Midnight Mass one cold and snowy Christmas

Eve. New buildings give me hope for the future. The businesses on Genesee Street gradually change but the Greene I see is like a painting by some artist who only paints what is picturesque. I will never cease to have a great affection for my hometown.

I wonder if anyone today has walked as many miles as I have throughout the village. How can anyone see all that I have seen from riding in a car? When I walked back and forth to work for eighteen years, I enjoyed the change of seasons and seeing the tiniest flowers spring forth in each flowerbed. I watched the progress of each renovation and new buildings going up. I enjoyed seeing babies born at our hospital become active children, then teenagers, and finally grow into adulthood. Once I moved to South Chenango Street, my 30-minute walks in the evening took me all over the village and I would think about the families who once lived on those streets and wonder what had become of them.

Bringing my family up in Greene was the best decision I could have made. I believe it was not only good for them, but it has been good for me as well. Living in a small town continues to be a blessing as I grow older. Friends stop by to visit me daily. When I am feeling poorly, I am overwhelmed at how concerned others are about me. Everyone is always so good to me.

Nineteen eighty-six was the year I set my mind on moving to the new Senior Citizens Residence under construction on Birdsall Street. I hoped that within six months there would be a buyer for my house and that I could dispose of everything that I would no longer need in an apartment. I started out by sorting out things in the cellar. The first day I came across old ledgers and diaries belonging to my father. I sat down to read those old diaries of Papa's and just could not throw them away. I knew I could not keep them so eventually gave them to Paul.

The task of sorting through historical records, family genealogies and personal belongings was overwhelming. I spent hours looking over things I had forgotten I had in my possession. I read bunches of letters Mama had saved from my nurses training days and from the Brooklyn Naval Hospital and early months of my marriage to Jimmy. There were letters Paul and I had written from 1927 to 1930 when we were in the West. I found them very interesting and there was so little that I wanted to discard. I re-read all of Tom and Jorette's letters that I had saved and they aroused many forgotten memories. Finally I spent days reading all my letters to the Professor and the 108 letters that he wrote to me. It was such fun reliving my life through all those old letters. Reading them was the tonic I needed to make scaling down my household belongings more agreeable.

It was a big relief when my house sold in November and I found buyers for furniture and appliances that I will no longer need. I gave away many family heirlooms to various members of my family. By the middle of December, I had gone through every drawer and closet and looked over the contents of every large envelope in my desk. I cannot remember any of my previous moves being this difficult. Fortunately, I was not alone in feeling overwhelmed. Mrs. Palmiter, my upstairs tenant, was going through the same thing that I was and we sought consolation in talking with each other while taking a short break.

Time moved along quickly that December. Jorette and I cleaned out my kitchen cupboards and packed boxes. Just before Christmas, I received a letter from CHIP (Chenango Housing Improvement Program) saying I could pick up the keys to my apartment, pay the first month's rent of $254 and move in the following Saturday.

Moving was more hectic than I imagined. One day, Jorette and Valerie helped pack small items and we made several trips to the apartment with boxes of fragile items, food, and plants. After one trip to the apartment, I forgot to take my house key, and we could not get back into my house. Neighbors and storekeepers tried to help us with all sorts of keys but not one fit any of my three doors. Finally my neighbor Marion Hayes pried the little pantry window up and we boosted her smallest daughter through it. It was a relief when Joanie let us into the house. All this took a lot of time and we were exhausted.

On December 27, 1986, the movers took everything to my upstairs apartment in the Village Greene Apartments. As soon as they departed, Jorette, Larry, and I set about unpacking and getting settled. I guess the excitement and stress was too much for me, as I felt lightheaded and had to lie down and just watch them unpack. It was quite a day for all of us.

Within five days, sixteen tenants had moved in and we had our first public gathering in the large foyer. We played cards, and I never saw so many refreshments. I believe I will enjoy living here.

\* \* \*

A year after my move to the Village Greene Apartments I wrote the following letter to my grandson Chris Cochrane.

*Dear Chris & Bev,*

*I am now living in a Senior Citizens Apartment House on Birdsall Street. It is a new home for seniors with thirty-three units, each containing a living room, kitchen, bedroom and bath. The living room has a double window facing east, perfect for my African violets. Of the thirty-three residents, there is but one man with his wife. The rest of us are widows, and many of us are in our 80s. I am going on 85 and still have all of my own teeth and almost no fillings, which is unusual for my age. I think it is because I grew up on a farm and drank raw milk.*

*We are a lively bunch. We play cards downstairs every evening. We don't care if we make mistakes; we just laugh. I don't think I have laughed so much in all my life as I have since I have been here. We play Pinochle and Pitch and it is such fun. Everyone is so friendly here.*

*We have frequent entertainment in our large community room by children and adult groups from the community. Once a week, we have Bible Study and occasional potluck suppers, movies, crafts, and parties. My brother lives a short distance from here and he drives me to church on Sundays, but I can easily walk to the beauty parlor, library, and stores.*

I continued to be active in my new surroundings for the next few years and was never at a loss for something to do. It was a wise decision to move into an apartment as I no longer worry about maintaining a house, shoveling the sidewalk in the winter or raking leaves in the fall. Life is simpler, but never dull. The main difference in my daily life is that it no longer holds the variety of activities and the unexpected happenings that have been a part of my life. I also miss having a purpose in life, which nursing, family, and historical research had provided throughout my lifetime.

I am fortunate to be able to take long walks with Evelyn Curtis when the weather is good. My latest hobbies are making baskets out of greeting cards and crocheting net scrubbers and my favorite pastime remains reading. I find some wonderful books at the public library, and am thankful my eyesight has not failed me. One of my friends takes me to the monthly Philomath meeting and my brother Paul takes me to church. I attend a weekly Bible Study at Bess Palmiter's apartment and occasionally go to the Aglow meetings at the Congregational Church. On Sundays, I watch my usual Christian programs on TV and never miss Billy Graham's crusades on television. Jorette visits me on Sunday afternoons and frequently takes me for a long ride over back roads to see the countryside that I love so dearly. Occasionally we stop to visit a relative or friend. Sometimes I stay overnight at her home and then Larry or DeeAhn will bring me home. Larry often drops by to visit and, oh, how I appreciate their frequent telephone calls. The girls here are great and we look out after one another. If I am not feeling well, someone will bring something for me to eat or check to see how I am before going to bed. There are few dull moments for me and I am content.

I attended a few Alumni Banquets over the years, but none that stands out in my mind as much as the one held at the Silo Restaurant in 1989. Three years earlier, the alumni had voted to hold future banquets on the Saturday evening before Labor Day, thinking this date would attract more alumni who might be visiting Greene for the holiday weekend. The 1989 banquet celebrated the 100th Anniversary of the founding of the Greene High School Alumni Association and more than 300 people attended the dinner. Larry escorted Jorette, DeeAhn, and me. It was such an honor when Ward Stanton introduced three members of my family who had all graduated from Greene High School. I graduated in 1920, Jorette in 1955, and DeeAhn in 1982. Harold Comfort and I were the oldest graduates in attendance. All of us saw many old acquaintances and enjoyed the evening immensely.

In 1991, DeeAhn, my twenty-five year old granddaughter, and I flew to California to visit Tom for a week. He met us at the San Francisco airport and from there drove to the Sea Ranch. DeeAhn and I both got carsick on that four-hour drive north on Highway 1. We had dinner at the Lodge one evening, where my grandson Chris was chef. We spent our last night at Susan Clark's home in Santa Rosa before flying home. I was so glad DeeAhn was with me, as I could never have made the trip by myself.

So many changes occurred in 1992 that it made my head swim. I was experiencing recurrent headaches on the left side of my head that left me weak and shaky. Occasionally neither Paul nor I felt well enough to go to church. On the first Sunday in February, Paul had a bad cold and felt so bad that he called Jorette to come and get him and take him to the hospital in Binghamton. The doctors immediately diagnosed pneumonia. I went to see Paul on Wednesday and he was responding to treatment, but a day later, he died—on February 7, 1992. He was 85. It was such a shock when Jorette, Larry, and DeeAhn came to tell me. Paul had confided in me that he had forgotten to have a pneumonia shot in the fall, and was sure that was the reason he had caught pneumonia. Jorette and Larry made all the arrangements for Paul's funeral, as I was unable to do anything. Tom arrived from California shortly before the funeral Mass. He spent a week helping Jorette and Larry go through all of Paul's belongings and deciding what to do with his house.

I was surprised at how much I missed Paul once he was gone. He had called me on the telephone regularly in the past few years and I missed hearing from him. We had celebrated nearly every major holiday together during the latter part of our lives and had learned to lean on each other after we each lived alone. For much of my life, I had been around people dying, but I admit that I do not like the burdens of old age, the slow decline in energy, and the pain of losing loved ones. Three weeks after Paul died, my close friend, Evelyn Curtis, became ill and her daughter moved her to Riverfront Centre in Binghamton. We had done so much together—watching television in the evenings, playing cards, and going to the library together. Without Paul and Evelyn, I felt alone for the first time in my life.

A month later, Tom returned to help Jorette and Larry paint the interior of Paul's house. There was a terrible ice storm followed by snow the day he arrived. I was thankful that his plane arrived safely. It was good having my family together and spending time with Tom as he worked at fixing up Paul's house. On Saturday evening, we four went to the Silo Restaurant for a Chamber of Commerce dinner where I was honored as Citizen of the Year. It was one of the happiest evenings of my life.

Not long after that, I decided that it would be best if I lived closer to Jorette and felt it was time to move into an assisted living facility. I asked Jorette to find out if there was an opening at the Riverfront Centre. There was an opening, so Jorette took me to visit Evelyn and to look the place over. I moved there on March 28. Evelyn and I immediately resumed watching TV together in the evenings and going for walks whenever the weather allowed.

# The Final Path Home

It was nice having my mother just minutes away from where we lived and comforting knowing that she and Evelyn were looking out for each other. However, she was slowing down and after the move to Binghamton, my mother "felt lost." Perhaps it was because she was in unfamiliar surroundings and missed looking out her window and seeing Greene. We took her up to our house as often as possible and went for rides in the country, which was something she always loved to do. Mother continued to be plagued with headaches, but the doctor could never pinpoint the cause or find a remedy.

Mother stopped writing in her diary a few months after her birthday in 1994. The entry for February 4 reads

*On my 90th birthday, Tom and his friend Susan Clark and Jorette and Larry and their family had a surprise birthday*

*celebration for me at a very nice restaurant in Binghamton. It was a bit overwhelming for me as I am unaccustomed to being fussed over.*

The last time that Mother and I went for a long walk was in June 1996. We walked down Front Street crossing the Riverside Drive Bridge, along the river to the Main Street Bridge and back to Riverfront Centre—a mile loop. The next day, Larry and I left for a Martin Family Reunion in Florida. The day before we returned home, Mom went for a walk with a friend. As she was crossing the driveway, she tripped and fell, breaking her hip and her right wrist in four places. Following surgery and three weeks in the hospital, Mother had to be moved to the Vestal Nursing Home. Once she recovered, and saw that she was in a hospital environment, she wanted to help and sometimes when I visited her, I would find her folding towels at the nurses' station. Her nature had always been to help others and although she was confined to a wheelchair, she could not sit idly by and watch other people busy at work without pitching in to give a helping hand.

Mother never wavered in maintaining her positive outlook on life. She had a peace about her that made the staff at the Vestal Nursing Home love her. She never ceased to remind me during my visits that "the best is yet to come." Her steadfast faith in Jesus assured her of eternal life and that when this life was over Jesus would gently call her home. She believed in the Word of God, that salvation is based on the finished work of Christ on Calvary—and she took God at His Word.

\* \* \*

Mildred took the final path to home on June 7, 1999, after being in a coma for eight days as a result of a stroke. As Larry and I stood by her bedside, watching her life ebb away, we willingly let her go on the final journey to her home in heaven. Was it a coincidence that the beautiful song "You'll Never Walk Alone" emanated from the cassette next to her bed at the moment of her death? As her spirit left the room, the poignant lyrics reflected her journey through life—that of absolute trust in the Lord.

# Author's Note

When I started to put this story of my mother's life together, it was with the intention of changing anything I wrote into third person. I intended to divide the book into two parts to separate my mother's earlier memoirs from what I *had* included. However, when I wrote in the third person, it was as if I was writing about another person, so I decided to leave everything in first person until the final chapter.

In going through boxes of old letters, I found one that my mother wrote to my father, in 1931, before they were married. She revealed her innermost thoughts in her letters. "I believe in destiny. Each event in our life happens for a purpose, no matter how terrible, how sad or how lovely. And it may be a long, long time before we come to know what that purpose is. Sometimes, it may be that we never know but can detect it in the lives of other people. It is like an endless chain. Nothing is ever taken from us but something else is given us in its stead and that which seems so vital and necessary one day can on the next day fade away into insignificance! So however badly we may want a thing if we do not get it I really believe it is best in the end that we should not."

In a letter to the Professor some twenty years later, she wrote, "I believe whatever happens is in the end, the best for us, however long it may take us to see it. It seems that when we release our worries there is a peace, which hitherto was not present. Each single circumstance, event and contact will dove-tail so perfectly that it really must be part of some great unseen Plan. Who can tell which is more the important role, the goal finally reached or the influences you, yourself, have made on others along the way. Life's great puzzle...so intricate. If we could only realize as we go along that nothing is unimportant, no word spoken, no deed performed however trivial, we would be very careful indeed. I wonder how anyone can deny the existence of a Supreme Being."

Mother had loads of perseverance and reliance on the Lord. She was no stranger doing without, due to her childhood experiences growing up on a farm in the early 1900s with no electricity and no running water, living through tough times during the Great Depression, and doing without in the war years. I believe she learned to be content in whatever circumstances she found herself in. She had learned that luxuries were not necessary in order to survive and that what we consider necessities are not what brings true happiness.

It was walking with God that developed the inner beauty of her character. My mother was a virtuous woman and surrendered both her work and family to God. She was devoted to our family yet was able to reach beyond that priority to accomplish other things as well. She was a stickler about good grammar and spelling. She never raised her voice with Tom or me and I never heard her say a swear word, not even an, *Oh, my God*!

In going through boxes of letters, which Mother saved throughout her lifetime, I came face to face with my real mother. It was like seeing her through another set of eyes. I came to see how her spiritual beliefs and nursing ethics ultimately defined her life. She loved her work and was a great example for her children—we learned to work at an early age and we learned that work is important. We understood that we played a part in making our family life run smoothly and we developed a sense of responsibility, which was due to the trust she placed in us.

Mother was never one to lounge around with nothing to do. She always had a project going as well as being an avid reader. She encouraged us to love books as a way to expand our horizons and to improve our minds. She loved poetry and collected quotations that spoke to her heart. The quotations found at the beginning of each chapter in this book are from a scrapbook that Mother started in 1919. She continued to jot down verses that spoke directly to her over the years. The ones I included in this book are from that brown scrapbook.

When my mother took on the role of town historian, I learned that she had an astonishing memory about the genealogy of the early settlers in Greene. Larry and I often remarked that those families were more real to her than the people she met on the street. She had an amazing knowledge of the history of Greene and fortunately was diligent in keeping records of everything. Today many of these records still exist as well as her two books on the history of Greene. When I recently returned to Greene to do some research, the one thing that jumped out at me is the affection and respect that people still hold for her today. To this end, Mother would have valued this far more than any award with her name on it, because she did not do anything for rewards. Everything my mother, Mildred, did was motivated by love.

# Epilogue

## by Thomas English Cochrane

Reading Mother's diaries, letters, and Jorette's accumulation of data and facts on our mother's life has given me a completely different viewpoint and appreciation of her life. In her life of ninety-five years, mother accomplished much more than I had any cognizance. Growing up, we spent really only 18 years with her and much of that was devoted to school, friends, and our own pursuits and establishing our own goals. In later life, I kept in touch but she talked little of her doings but wanted to know about our lives and the children.

I saw my mother as a modest, soft-spoken woman. She talked little of her accomplishments, travels, past life, and her future goals. She instead pushed us to do things and develop our own goals. She valued education, pushed us to achieve in school. She read to us when we were little children and introduced us to the Public Library by age seven. I don't think she particularly valued sports, although she did encourage us to do well in whatever we decided to undertake.

We were raised Roman Catholics and attended Mass every Sunday. I recall little specific discussion of Catholicism, but she instilled in us her moral values of integrity, truthfulness, honor, loyalty, forgiveness, respect, and being kind to others. I never heard her speak a bad word about anyone else. She focused on the positive, rather than the negative. Her religious beliefs were personal but she stressed to us that saying our prayers each night was something we should do.

Jorette and I were given responsibilities at a young age of six or seven. Mother worked as a nurse and ran the local hospital, so she had gone to work before we left in the morning for school or she arrived home after we were out of school. We learned to take care of the house, do the cooking, much of the cleaning, and even the washing of clothes. I don't remember ironing, but I don't do much now either. I guess I grew up wrinkled! However, the rules were simple—we never left the house with an unmade bed, no clothes on the floor, and no unwashed dishes in the sink. The lights were all off and the doors locked. We were supposed to be neat and presentable and have our homework done. She rarely asked us if our homework was done—it was just expected! We did not wear jeans or dirty or ragged clothes to school.

Mother took pleasure in growing flowers and spent her time off weeding and planting flowerbeds. We helped her with pruning and weeding. We also grew a garden and I think Jorette and I were the primary keepers of the garden. We raised strawberries and sold some of them. Jorette was into raising gladiolas. Mother did have time for canning and freezing of fruits and vegetables.

When Jorette and I became teenagers, Mother thought we should be introduced to travel vacations and prior to our driving years, we took bus trips to New England, Niagara Falls, New York City, and the Adirondacks. We were introduced to Revolutionary War history and places, which later sparked our own interests in history.

My mother encouraged me to have a close relationship with her brother during my growing up years. Uncle Paul was shorter than Mother and tended to be stocky. He grew up learning to work hard on Grandpa's farm and was quite strong for a man of his size. He had a trapeze bar and barbells in his attic and he regularly worked out. When I was a boy, Uncle Paul tried to teach me to "skin the cat" on the bar. I could never do it, but he could do all sorts of trapeze tricks on that bar. Uncle Paul liked to tinker and would work for hours trying to repair or design something. He did not work on car engines but did work on small engines for his motor cycles and motor boats. He taught me how to repair my bicycle and other things, taught me some mathematical calculations, and how to fish and hunt.

Uncle Paul was an avid fisherman, loved the Chenango River, and was very respectful of our environment. He never left trash or dumped trash carelessly. He and my grandfather always put down farmers who left junk everywhere. He loved hunting small game and going deer hunting. He hunted woodchucks with a passion, because when he was young, horses sometimes stepped in a woodchuck hole and broke a leg. Long after tractors replaced horses, Uncle Paul and I spent many afternoons hunting woodchucks. If we killed other small animals or birds, we had to eat them. He could sit forever and wait for a woodchuck or a squirrel to raise its head. I learned to sit for long periods with him while hunting or fishing with little or no conversation or noise.

Mother was happy that Paul took such an interest in me and never worried about me when I was hanging out with him. He was a loyal booster of the Greene High School athletic teams and attended every football game and many of my wrestling matches. Uncle Paul was very good to me and I learned a lot from him.

Mother's interest in the local history of Greene and genealogy did not really develop until we were near graduation from high school. I do remember taking her around to cemeteries and other town libraries in my early driving years. Most of her extensive work, research and her two books were completed after I left home.

I don't recall being around when she gave a talk on local history or nursing. She seemed to me as almost too shy to be a public speaker. I wish that I had been there to hear her. Mother had a zest for life; she overcame the bad times with work, devotion to hobbies, and staying involved in other people's lives.

—Her son, Tom Cochrane